WHERE THE FAULT LIES

Why African American Marriages Are In Crisis

SHARON D. DOMINGUEZ

What others are saying about this book:

"*Where The Fault Lies...*, is a work that has been ordained by God. It can be used to demonstrate the biblical principles necessary to strengthen the Christian marriage, and it draws on the history, culture and spirituality of Black people. It identifies concrete and vivid life experiences that provide powerful vehicles for the Church's teaching ministry. Sharon Dominguez deserves our thanks!"
– **Leon Perry, III. Senior Pastor, Metropolitan Community Church—Chicago, Illinois.**

"This is the best bridge between the social/spiritual yoke of slavery to the promises in God's word that I have seen concerning marriage."
– **Michelle Aikens, Founder and CEO of Sepia Prime Woman Digital Magazine, Chicago, Illinois**

"Dr. Sharon Dominguez's book, *Where The Fault Lies*, gives its reader an insightful historical exploration that provides an in depth understanding of the root causes of marital and family breakdown, and a solution for newfound oneness, restoration, and freedom from bondage. The structure of this book makes it a very flexible "must have" resource for individuals, couples, families, institutions, professionals, study groups, and anyone else in search of the truth that makes us all free."
– **Tony McClain, Vice President, Jeneca Consulting, Oak Brook, Illinois**

"Dr. Dominguez has touched a vital nerve of our society in her book, '*Where The Fault Lies: Why African-American Marriages Are In Crisis.*' This book provides a historical basis for this crisis, and then provides solid direction for change in the home and in our society. It is true that "As the home goes, so goes the nation," and if our nation is to change, then the home must be strengthened."
– **Dr. Russell Kopp, President, Regency Christian College, Jacksonville, Florida.**

"Where The Fault Lies is an important read on American history. It truly sheds the light on the deep scars from slavery that continue to haunt the black family. A great read!"
– **J. Wells, President, Bonzi Entertainment, Beverly Hills, California**

"Where the Fault Lies,...is an in-depth look into the complex paradox that sometimes destroys the delicate fabric that binds together the relationships between men and women. The book offers keen insight of how to avoid the pitfalls that unfortunately claims too often many marriages in today's society."
– **Terrance Barker, Esq., Terrance Barker Legal Services, Country Club Hills, Illinois**

"FINALLY! God inspired insight, with practical truths...Where The Fault Lies will equip you to effectively take a stand for Marriage and the Family, understanding the dynamics and destructive forces set against the original design of God ordained marriage. May hope spring forth in your heart as it did in mine, causing you to know that New Beginnings can Spring Forth from old ruins."
– **LaTonya F. James, Executive Director, Sapphire Ministries International**

"A thought provoking, yet necessary exposure to historical influences that have negatively shaped present-day African-American relationships and marriages. In similar fashion to eradicating any social inequity, the problem must be acknowledged; its impact measured; and causative agents removed for community survival. This forward thinking is clearly evident in Where the Fault Lies."
– **Deana M. Newman, M.P.H., C.C.P., Cardiovascular, Perfusionist, Grand Ledge, Michigan**

"Dr Dominguez takes us on a journey of self discovery. This is true synergy, mother wit and wisdom woven together and made available in a comprehensive work. One plus one is more than two in this masterpiece! In setting the historical context, line upon line, precept upon precept, this writing is a must for those who want immediate results. Full of can't miss, user friendly insights, it's an easy read for those looking for answers to their prayers, young and getting older, those that are married and those that want to be. Excellent in Arabic - MUNTAZ!!!"
– **Albert L Koger III, Associate Pastor, Grace Outreach Church, Riyadh The Kingdom of Saudi Arabia**

WHERE THE FAULT LIES

SHARON D. DOMINGUEZ

WHERE THE FAULT LIES:
WHY AFRICAN-AMERICAN MARRIAGES ARE IN CRISIS
By Sharon D. Dominguez
Published by, *God In Charge Accessories*
"Accessories for the Kingdom"
P.O. Box 6183 Sun City Center, FL 33571-6183

Scriptures quotations marked (NIV) are taken from the *Holy Bible, New International Version*®. *NIV*®. Copyright © 1973, 1978, 1984 by the International Bible Society. Used by permission of Zondervan Publishing House. All rights reserved.

Scriptures quotations marked (NKJV) are taken from the new King James Version. Copyright © 1982 by Thomas Nelson, Inc. Used by permission. Scripture quotations marked (NASB) are taken from the New American Standard Bible. Copyright © The Lockman Foundation, 1960, 62, 63, 68, 71, 73, 75, 77. All rights reserved. Scripture quotations marked (KJV) are taken from the King James Version.

Scripture quotations marked (TLB) are taken from the Living Bible, Copyright © 1971, and scripture quotations marked (NLT) are taken from the Holy Bible, New Living Translation, Copyright © 1996. Used by permission of Tyndale House Publishers, Inc., Wheaton, Illinois 60189. All rights reserved.

Italics in Scripture quotations reflect the author's added emphasis.

Editor: Chuck Vermillion, HelpPublish.com

Cover and book design: Yvonne Vermillion, MagicGraphix.com

Copyright © 2004 by Sharon D. Dominguez

All rights reserved. No part of this book may be reproduced or transmitted in any form or by any means without express written consent of the publisher.

Printed in the United States of America

2nd printing 2014

ISBN 10: 0-9748397-0-1

ISBN 13: 978-0974839707

Library of Congress Control Number: 2003116115

Cover photo courtesy of The Vivian G. Harsh Research Collection of Afro-American History and Literature, Chicago Public Library.

Grateful acknowledgements are made to the following for permission to reprint previously published material:

THE BLACK FAMILY IN SLAVERY AND FREEDOM, 1750-1925 by Herbert Gutman, Copyright © 1976 by Herbert G. Gutman. Used by permission of Pantheon Books, a division of Random House, Inc.

SLAVE TESTIMONY: TWO CENTURIES OF LETTERS, SPEECHES, INTERVIEWS, AND AUTOBIOGRAPHIES, edited by John W. Blassingame. Copyright © 1977 by Louisiana State University Press. Reprinted by permission of Louisiana State University Press.

DEAR ONES AT HOME: LETTERS FROM THE CONTRABAND CAMPS, edited by Henry L. Swint Copyright © 1966 By Vanderbilt University Press. Reprinted by permission of Vanderbilt University Press.

OH HOW I VISION, by Brian Lee Copyright © 1996. Used by permission.

Dedication

To those individuals who have shared with me the personal struggles in their marriages, and in so doing, have inspired me to search for answers.

TABLE OF CONTENTS

INTRODUCTION
FOR A TIME SUCH AS THIS: STATING THE CASE FOR AFRICAN-AMERICAN MARRIAGES.................. 1

PART I
DISCOVERING THE FAULT LINE

A LOOK AT HISTORY.................. 13

I. AN OPEN DOOR: SLAVERY 17
II. POINT OF ENTRY: THE SLAVE MARRIAGE.................. 23
III. A SPIRITUAL ASSAULT: FORCED TERMINATION.................. 35
IV. CAUGHT IN THE CROSSFIRE: GRIEVING WITH GOD FOR THE CHILDREN.................. 49
V. PSYCHOLOGICAL WARFARE: THE PSYCHOLOGICAL EFFECTS ON WOMANHOOD AND MANHOOD.................. 59
VI. SAFE HOUSES: "SPIRITUAL SONGS".................. 67

THE END OF SLAVERY.................. 77

PART II.
AFTERSHOCKS

THE IMPACT OF SLAVERY ON TODAY'S COUPLE.................. 81

VII. BROKEN IMAGES: STEREOTYPES THAT DESTROY ONENESS.... 85
VIII. OPTING FOR FREEDOM: A WORD ON DELIVERANCE... 93

PART III
RESTORING THE FOUNDATION

A PROPHETIC PROCLAMATION.................. 99

IX. A SPIRIT OF REFORM: LEARNING TO LOVE GOD'S WAY.........103
X. BUILDING SAFE HOUSES: MENTORING AFRICAN-AMERICAN COUPLES.................. 115

CONCLUSION
SOUL FOOD: BREAKING BREAD WITH THE KING.............. 121

RESOURCES FOR KINGDOM BUILDING:
RECOMMENDATIONS FROM THE AUTHOR

FOREWORD

There is a war going on and the casualties are mounting. One would think that I am talking about the war in the natural. But no, I am talking about the spiritual war, this war being fought against the kingdom of darkness, against the Kingdom of Light.

And as this war is being waged in the spiritual, it is manifesting in the natural. And there is no greater fight than in the marriage area.

We are now seeing an alarming rate of Christian marriages that are being tried, terminated, and ending tragically. But there is hope, in one of the most thought provoking and analyzing books to come out in many years, "Where The Fault Lies," written by Prophetess Sharon D. Dominguez.

In her first book, Sharon has dealt with the attack on marriage especially from an African-American historical viewpoint. She thoroughly analyzes the effect that slavery had, and is still having on the institution of marriage.

I have not read a book that not only gives historical roots, but also biblical medicine to marriages in crises. Even though it was written from an African-American perspective, it is a healing balm for marriages of all ethnics. I highly recommend "Where The Fault Lies" to you, not only if your marriage is healthy, but for you to minister to those that are not.

I pray that those who read this book will gain insight, wisdom, and strength, but also strategies for fighting the enemy in his attack on the covenant of marriages.

In Him,
Apostle H. Daniel Wilson

*For how can I bear to see the calamity
that is coming on my people?
Or how can I bear to see the destruction
of my kindred?
(Esther 8:6, NASB)*

INTRODUCTION

FOR A TIME SUCH AS THIS: STATING THE CASE FOR AFRICAN-AMERICAN MARRIAGE

Marriage is an ordained institution blessed by the hand of God. The institution of marriage was set in Genesis 2:24, *"For this reason a man will leave his father and mother and be united to his wife, and they will become one flesh" (NIV)*. This divine plan of God set into motion God's Will for His people, giving us a portrait of Christ's love for His church. Today, there is a painful picture that is being painted for our Nation's marriages. One author describes this trend best:

"...a cultural sledgehammer has attacked the American family..."

> "In the past four decades, a cultural sledgehammer has attacked the American family, and the evidence of collateral damage is everywhere. Since 1960, the number of couples getting married has declined by one-third, while the number of couples getting divorced has more than doubled. In 1994, for the first time in American history, divorce replaced death as the principal cause of family dissolution."[1]

WHERE THE FAULT LIES: WHY AFRICAN-AMERICAN MARRIAGES ARE IN CRISIS

This picture clearly shows the spiritual attack that has been waged against marriage. The media, talk radio, and even casual conversation will confirm the rising statistics of marital disruption in the United States. What is particularly disturbing is that African-American marriages have been hit the hardest with many of its marriages ending in divorce. Since the 1960s, scholars have been concerned with the rising divorce rate in the African-American community. There have even been debates in our churches, universities, and in government over the survival of the African-American family.

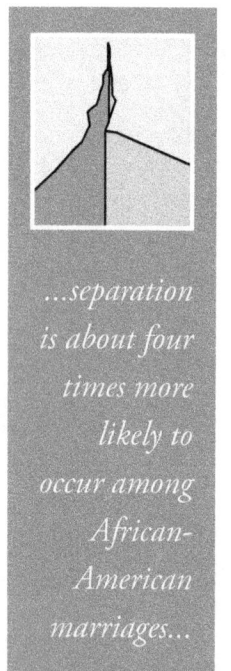

...separation is about four times more likely to occur among African-American marriages...

Marriage patterns among African-Americans have long revealed a trend of *leading* the divorce rate, even if by a small margin. In earlier times, even though marriages were stronger, African-American women would experience marital disruption much more often than others would. Before 1960, studies showed that figures were unreliable because of permanent separations not reported as divorce, and informal divorce agreements. After 1960, separations were also widely found in the African-American community.[2] For example, as implied by the separation and divorce rates between 1965 and 1979, within ten years of the wedding, 47 percent of Black married women would separate from their husbands.[3]

This gloomy forecast continued into the 1990s. According to researchers Douglas Besharov and Andrew West, separation is about four times more likely to occur among African-American marriages than among Whites, and about one and a half times more likely than among Hispanics. In 1998, of married Black women aged fifteen and over, more than 20 percent had an absent spouse, in comparison with 5 percent of married White women and 13 percent among Hispanic women of the same ages.[4]

To explain these startling statistics, "socioeconomic ills" became the suspected culprit. However, the conclusions and scholarly answers have not stopped the disruption. African-American marriages are more likely to end in divorce than in the general population.[5]

Whether it is a long-standing separation, divorce, or both, the high incidence of marital disruption is evident. What is going to happen to our families if we continue at this rate? A glimpse of the family in the twenty-first century can be seen in recent census statistics. There were 8.8 million Black families in the U.S. in 2002, and nearly one-half (48 percent) were two parent families, 43 percent of these Black families were headed by women with no husband present, and 9 percent were headed by Black men with no wife present.[6]

My heart aches as I see the calamity heading toward our families.

Certainly, there are strong viable Black marriages that have exemplified the standard of a Godly union. They have been an inspiration to all who want to achieve a lifetime of oneness and happiness in marriage. But today there is a visible stronghold choking the life from African-American marriages. My heart aches as I see the calamity heading toward our families. How should the people of God be responding to this crisis? As we turn to the bible, there is a clear illustration seen in the Book of Esther, as to how we should respond.

"A COMMUNITY IN CRISIS"

The conflict in Chapters 3 and 4 of the book of Esther, between Haman the Agagite and Mordecai the Jew, set the stage for a race of people to be put into "crisis". In the twelfth year of King Xerxes, Haman, a government official, wanted to destroy all the Jewish people. Haman's fury was ignited when he was told that one of the king's servants (Mordecai the Jew) refused to bow in obeisance to him. Haman wanted more than personal vengeance, so he developed a scheme to destroy Mordecai and his people. Haman set the case before the king in verse 8. He explains:

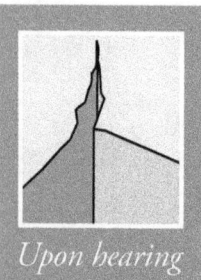

Upon hearing the news, Mordecai tore his clothing, dressed himself in the traditional sackcloth, and sprinkled himself with ashes

...*There is a certain race of people scattered through all the provinces of your empire. Their laws are different from those of any other nation, and they refuse to obey even the laws of the king. So it is not in the king's interest to let them live...issue a decree that they be destroyed. (Esther 3:8, NLT)*

The king agreed, and unknowingly sealed the Jews' fate with his ring. Haman, excited about the coming execution, dictated letters to all the local officials in each province. The signed letters described a death warrant for all Jews. Upon hearing the news, Mordecai tore his clothing, dressed himself in the traditional sackcloth, and sprinkled himself with ashes. Although, he was bitterly grief-stricken, he hit the city streets and made his way to the palace.

While word spread, the Jewish people learned of their impending fate, and panic and confusion broke out in the land. Imagine the turmoil, chaos, and mass confusion it caused in the family unit, in not understanding why your family had to die. Along with this was the psychological warfare, since the impending executions were not to be held until a year later. As the news traveled, there was great sorrow among the Jews. There was weeping, wailing, and the adornment of sackcloth to show their grief. Many Jews fasted, as was their custom. In the Old Testament, people would often fast in response to calamity in order to focus on God. In any case, their response was collective. They took the threat to their families seriously enough to act!

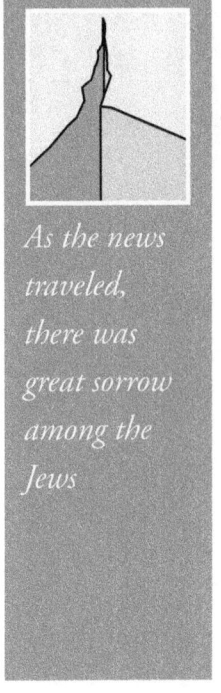

As the news traveled, there was great sorrow among the Jews

As Mordecai reached the palace gates, he was not permitted to enter. This was due to his sad countenance and sackcloth attire. Queen Esther's maids informed her of Mordecai's condition. Queen Esther was so disturbed by her cousin's mourning, that it prompted her to send him a change of clothing. When Mordecai refused the clothing, Queen Esther sent word for him to reveal the nature of his grief. Mordecai explained the grave situation and pleaded with Queen Esther to appear before the King to ask for mercy for her people. She responds by telling Mordecai that it would be impossible. She reminds him that it would be unlawful to appear before the King uninvited. Mordecai quickly reminded her that she too would not miss the fate of the Jewish people if she so refused. With this reminder, Queen Esther conceded and appealed to the King. In the end, Haman was executed and by the king's decree, the Jews were allowed to defend themselves. They united and defeated their enemy.

Like this biblical example, one must also take the threat to African-American families seriously. We too can defeat the enemy. The saints of God have been given permission to defend themselves. In the defense, the case for African-American marriages has already been stated, but one must know who should be prosecuted. The verdict is in, and the guilty party is revealed in Ephesians 6:12, *"for we wrestle not against flesh and blood, but against principalities, against powers, against the rulers of the darkness of this world, against spiritual wickedness in high places" (KJV).* The arrest is executed through 2 Corinthians 10:4, *"For the weapons of our warfare are not carnal, but mighty through God to the pulling down of strong holds" (KJV).* "Strongholds" are torn down when we seek to understand and grow in the wisdom of God. *"Through wisdom a house is built, And by understanding, it is established" (Proverbs 24:3, NKJV).*

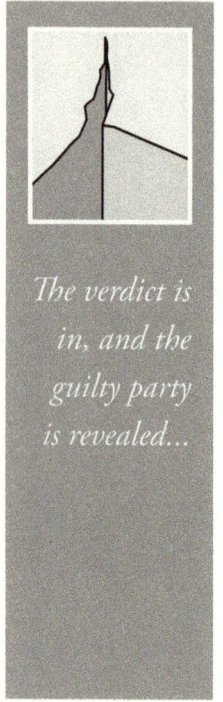

The verdict is in, and the guilty party is revealed...

Initially, Queen Esther did not ask Mordecai why he was mourning. Evidently, she thought it would be wise to send a change of clothing. Her purpose is unclear as to whether she wanted him to stop his wailing, or to provide him with proper clothing to enter the palace. If the latter is the case, gaining entrance into the palace to speak directly to Queen Esther seemed less important to the moral stance he was trying to demonstrate. Changing his outer garment would have been only a temporary "cover-up", and it would not have solved the problem. His outer garment was an outward display of his inner turmoil and brokenness. His refusal to change clothing sparked a request for more information.

Asking for more information when we do not have all the facts opens the door to a greater understanding. The Lord says,

WHERE THE FAULT LIES: WHY AFRICAN-AMERICAN MARRIAGES ARE IN CRISIS

"My people are destroyed for lack of knowledge..." (Hosea 4:6, KJV). To ignore the issue would have meant certain death for the Jewish people. *"...Yes, a man of knowledge increases strength..." (Proverbs 24:5, NKJV).* Mordecai explicitly explained the upcoming holocaust being planned for the Jewish people. He shared the decree and exposed the plan. Initially, Queen Esther had some reservations about what she was expected to do with the information. But through wise counsel, Queen Esther came to understand that the decree might certainly apply to her as well. As a result, she agreed to petition the king and to intercede to save the Jewish people. *"For by wise counsel you will wage your own war..." (Proverbs 24:6, NKJV).*

We need more than scholars weeping and wailing about this crisis.

In this hour, one must ask the question, why are African-Americans mourning the death of so many marriages? Could the outer garment of divorce be an outward display of a deeper issue? We need more than scholars weeping and wailing about this crisis. Although Mordecai and the Jewish people were collectively concerned, it was not enough to save the Jewish race. It took someone who had been divinely positioned behind the Palace walls to intercede for the people.

For A Time Such As This, the people of God have been set in the Kingdom to intercede for African-American marriages.

Queen Esther was determined to save the lives of her people. She said, "If I perish, I perish." We must be willing to take on the spiritual fight for the future of our families. A protective hedge has to be built, and a war has to be waged to help free troubled marriages. To increase strength, the battle plan has to be strategically developed with information that is crucial to the success of its mission.

WHERE THE FAULT LIES: WHY AFRICAN-AMERICAN MARRIAGES ARE IN CRISIS

The mission to save African-American marriages must include an understanding from an historical perspective, not to find fault, but to discover key areas of spiritual vulnerability. Historical research is necessary when an intercessory group is prompted by the Holy Spirit to attack strongholds over a city or a region. "Strongholds" leave telltale signs through historical evidence. As an offensive plan, it is crucial to have an historical perspective along with understanding the current stressors that may add to normal marital conflict. Our arsenal must include literary weapons that replace lies with truth, and the lack of knowledge with the knowledge and wisdom of God. All in all, this study will provide the information that is needed to wage your own war against the destruction of African-American marriages.

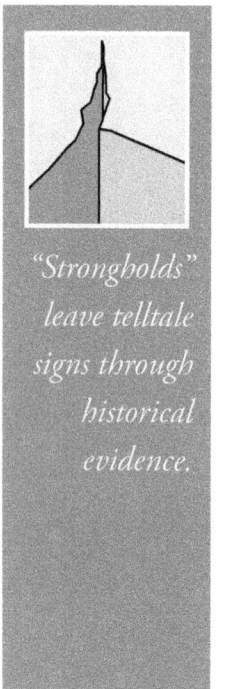

"Strongholds" leave telltale signs through historical evidence.

QUESTIONS FOR REFLECTION AND DISCUSSION

1. Why do you think African-Americans are mourning the death of so many marriages?

2. For a time such as this, what contribution do you feel your spiritual gift will make in the appeal to save African-American marriages?

DISCOVERING THE FAULT LINE

PART I

Clasping each other by the hand, pledging our sacred honor that we would be true, we called on high heaven to witness the rectitude of our purpose. There was nothing that could be more binding upon us as slaves than this; for marriage among American slaves, is disregarded by the laws of this country.

HENRY BIBB, FORMER SLAVE—1849

If the foundations are destroyed, what can the righteous do?
         (Psalm 11:3, KJV)

A LOOK AT HISTORY

$\mathcal{B}$eneath the Earth's surface lie fractures in the Earth's crust caused by shifting in the Earth's tectonic plates. These breaks or faults lie mainly hidden from natural sight. Although hidden to society, these fractures set up the potential for Earthquakes in the future. The fault line serves as the original marker of where the initial break in the foundation took place. Although future eruptions may not occur for centuries, the build-up creates tension beneath the surface that may cause the fault to snap. In the end, fault lines leave evidence of a vulnerable place in the Earth's surface.

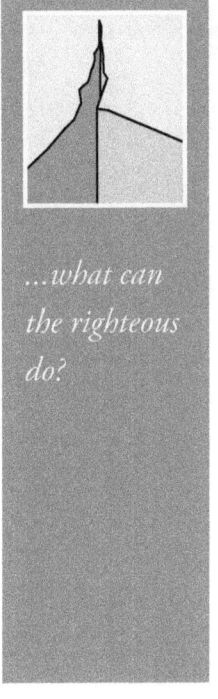

...what can the righteous do?

Seemingly, there is an *historical* fault line in the crust of the African-American culture. The foundation of the African-American family appears to have *shifted* as a result of slavery. The foundation is important, and whether it is a foundation for a house, political system, or culture, the word "foundation" establishes the structure and its components. In Psalm 11:3, the foundation is in question. King David's advisors are less than optimistic about King David's safety, so they ask him the question, *"If the foundations are destroyed, what can the righteous do?"* (Psalm 11:3, KJV). The word "foundations" in the Hebrew means, "basis, moral support, or purpose."[1] What was the basis of their fear, and how was the moral support diminished? Although the foundation of the African-American family was not destroyed, the implications of a

WHERE THE FAULT LIES: WHY AFRICAN-AMERICAN MARRIAGES ARE IN CRISIS

massive attempt to destroy the basis, moral support, and purpose for the African-American family can be seen in American history. With the establishment of institutionalized slavery, an organized attempt was made to eliminate the human needs of all Blacks, free and slave.

The early development of the slave family denied couples traditional male/female roles in their unions. For men, the role of a husband and father was circumvented. He could offer his family no protection or provision. Slavery also challenged womanhood in slave wives. They participated in strenuous labor, birthed and cared for several children, cooked, and cleaned. She was also physically abused and had to meet the sexual advances from slaveholders. Slave couples were also sold away to new owners and forced to marry mates of their masters' choice. Nevertheless, in spite of this insidious treatment, slave couples continued to fall in love and commit to marriage.

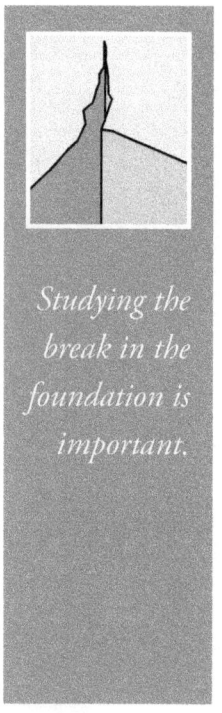

Studying the break in the foundation is important.

However, these troubled beginnings of African-American marriages appear to have created an "historical" fault, which lies dormant and waiting to erupt in marriages all over the nation. Studying the break in the foundation is important. Being aware of the areas of conflict that lead couples to divorce is essential in saving marriages. Therefore, given these points the examination of chattel slavery is a starting point in understanding the dynamics that threaten the stability of African-American marriages.

QUESTIONS FOR REFLECTION AND DISCUSSION

1. What evidence of the "historical fault" have you observed in African American marriages today?

2. Research the scripture text surrounding Psalm 11:3. What was David's response to their question?

3. The word "foundations" in the Hebrew means basis, purpose, and moral support. In light of this definition, are African-American couples questioning their *purpose*? If so, what is the *basis* of their fear? And how has the *moral support* been diminished?

For they are My servants, whom I brought out of the land of Egypt; they shall not be sold as slaves. You shall not rule over him with rigor, but you shall fear your God.
(Leviticus 25:42-43, NKJV)

- I -
AN OPEN DOOR: SLAVERY

Slavery, according to Webster's Dictionary, is a condition in which one person is owned by another. Consequently, the slave is forced to obey a master. The roots of slavery are found in ancient times. From the time of Abraham, the Hebrew patriarchs had slaves, or were slaves themselves. Slavery was practiced by every ancient civilization known to man. It was a part of the culture for many civilizations, such as the Egyptians, Romans, Sumerians, Assyrians, Babylonians, Syrians, Moabites, and countless others. Slaves had the lowest social status, if any, and yet were essential to the economic stability of their owners. As time evolved, slavery continued to survive in early European civilizations and in Africa.[1]

Slaves had the lowest social status, if any, and yet were essential to the economic stability of their owners.

Although slavery was common, slaves in Africa did not experience the horrific trials experienced in the Americas. Slavery in Africa was a result of defeat in war. Many victors chose to enslave their captives instead of killing them. The rationale was that the captives had been outwitted and overpowered. Other captives were being enslaved as punishment for criminal acts. One major difference between African and American slavery, was that slaves and slave owners in Africa were part of the same race, and therefore looked like their captors. They did not consider them inferior by birth. They were accustomed to the food, language, and the way of life. In this way, they were not introduced to a foreign world. The slaves also worked under the same conditions as their captors, except that they lacked status in the community. Many worked as servants or farm laborers.²

In Africa, slaves might have held the lowest status in society, but slavery on their home continent meant race was irrelevant, and slaves were considered as human as other workers. Slaves were not just property, but could improve their standing by their service, and could feel secure in knowing that their children could not be taken away from them and sold.³ Although this was true in most cases, not all African-owned slaves received these considerations. Slave life differed from region to region and from master to master.⁴

The slave merchants would use any means necessary to gain access to new slaves.

For the most part, slavery in Africa was widespread and well established before Europeans reached their shores in the early 1500s. During this time, the trading of human beings in exchange for material goods got its start. Some slaves were sold outright for violating African law, while others were sold as prisoners of war. The plantation market in the West Indies, North America, and Brazil placed a demand on the economy for more slaves between 1700 and 1850. Therefore, slave raids became a common occurrence on the coast of Africa. The slave merchants would use any means necessary to gain access to new slaves.⁵

In the book, *Equiano's Travels*, we find the description of a common slave raid, experienced by an eleven-year-old boy, Olaudah Equiano. Olaudah has on many days served as lookout to protect his father's village-kingdom of Essaka, Benin. There was always a danger of other Africans raiding for slaves. On several occasions, Equiano and his fellow guards had even captured slave hunters and had brought them before his father.

WHERE THE FAULT LIES: WHY AFRICAN-AMERICAN MARRIAGES ARE IN CRISIS

"One day, when all our people were gone out to their work as usual, and only I and my sister were left to mind the house, two men and a woman got over our walls, and in a moment seized us both... Without giving us time to cry out, or to make any resistance, they stopped our mouths and ran off with us into the nearest wood. Here they tied our hands, and continued to carry us as far as they could."[6]

In the following months, Equiano was sold many times over from trader to trader.

Slavery was dominated by corrupt individuals and practices. From the 15th to the 19th centuries, as the call for slaves in Europe and eventually America grew, the African slave trade increased in breadth and became much more brutal.[7] The Atlantic slave trade created such wealth that Europeans came to label Africans as "black gold".[8] The trading practice was a vicious cycle of selling men for the profit of other men.

As the slave trade continued, African slaves became regarded as chattel. Chattel describes a person regarded as a fixed item of personal property. Unlike slavery in Africa, race became the "badge of slavery". "The slave's heaviest chain was the color of his skin."[9] By the 18th century, slave codes made slavery involuntary and hereditary.[10]

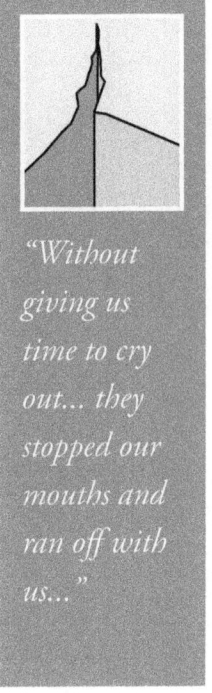

"Without giving us time to cry out... they stopped our mouths and ran off with us..."

The slave trade flourished with little opposition. Churchmen gave license to slavery by representing it as a crusade against pagans. Slave traders argued that the trade would rid Africa of unwanted criminals.[11] In the 1700s, "The church used Biblical authority to depict Africans as bearers of the Mark of Cain and as Children of Ham, cursed by Noah to be the "servants of servants".[12] In one respect, this type of reasoning made slavery moral in the eyes of the people, but some conscientious churchmen grappled with the idea of owning another man.

One such religious group was known as the Society of Friends, or Quakers. This group insisted that slavery conflicted with Christian morals. Throughout the years of slavery, they were instrumental in initiating several bills and petitions to outlaw slavery.[13]

Not all Africans that were brought to the Americas were brought in chains. Some Africans initially were held as indentured servants. An indentured servant made contracts, often an exchange of labor for passage to America. They served for a limited time, commonly seven years, and upon finishing their indenture they generally received "freedom dues", which was often land and clothing.[14] The book of Deuteronomy reveals a law concerning this type of contract:

Churchman gave license to slavery by representing it as a crusade against pagans.

> *If your brother, a Hebrew man, or a Hebrew woman, is sold to you and serves you six years, then in the seventh year you shall let him go free from you. And when you send him away free from you, you shall not let him go away empty-handed; you shall supply him liberally from your flock, from your threshing floor, and from your wine-press. From what the Lord has blessed you with, you shall give to him.*
> *(Deuteronomy 15:12-14, NKJV)*

By 1650, there were an estimated 300 indentured servants in the American colonies. But by the end of the seventeenth century, all Africans brought into the New World were declared slaves.[15]

QUESTIONS FOR REFLECTION AND DISCUSSION

1. Write three interesting facts that you learned from this section.

2. How was the word of God used to justify chattel slavery in the United States?

And He answered and said to them, "Have you not read that He who made them at the beginning made them male and female." and said, "For this reason a man shall leave his father and mother and be joined to his wife, **and the two shall become one flesh?"**
(Matthew 19:4, 5, NKJV)

- II -
POINT OF ENTRY:
THE SLAVE MARRIAGE

The slave community was not allowed to legally marry. Chattel slavery set up a system where slaves were not free agents, and they could not enter into a legal contract. The Southern legal system would not acknowledge slave marriages, on the grounds that "property can not enter into a legal contract." In 1858, a North Carolina judge states: "with slaves, it may be dissolved at the pleasure of either party, or by the sale of one or both, depending on the caprice or necessity of the owners."[1] The master-slave relationship took on a higher order than relationships between slaves. The relationships for free men and women could not be compared to the relationships between slaves and other slaves, or between a free man and his property. The people would not consider a law that would hinder them from selling their property.[2]

The Southern legal system would not acknowledge slave marriages...

The slaveholder held a disregard for the natural divine order of marriage. Many marriages were created on the sole whim of the master. He would order the slaves into two lines and beckon the male slaves to choose a wife from the opposite line. Then he would announce that they were married. Other masters placed male slaves with women whom they believed to be ready for childbearing. To acknowledge a union, some White clergymen presided at slave marriages, but they usually omitted from the ceremony the phrases, "until death do us part," and, "let no man put asunder," for they knew that the master might sell the husband away from his wife, or wife from husband."[3]

As time went on, some slaveholders became more lenient in allowing their slaves to take part in their marriage decision-making. At the same time, as African customs met with American influences, a unique courtship developed among the slaves. This involved a prescribed etiquette that used figurative speech as a test of wit. This verbal pursuit included asking a series of questions to seek out a possible mate. Slave men felt that, "the slave girl had to be won as surely as did her fair young mistress, and her black fellow in slavery, who aspired to her hand, had to prove his worthiness to receive it."[4] Therefore, young men initiated their courtship with fine speeches and soft poetic words.

Young men spent time developing and memorizing their poems in hopes of winning the woman of their dreams. One ex-slave fondly remembered "Uncle Gilbert", a shoemaker who was experienced in the art of courtship. It was to his shop that the slave men went for instruction in the ways of winning a mate. When a man was seeking to woo a maiden, a man might engage himself in this type of courtship conversation:

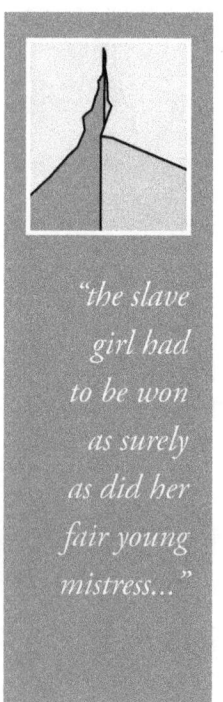

"the slave girl had to be won as surely as did her fair young mistress..."

He: My dear kin' miss, has you any objections to me drawing my cher to yer side, and revolvin' de wheel of my conversation around de axle of your understanding?

She: I has no objection to a gentleman addressin' me in a proper manner, kin' sir.

WHERE THE FAULT LIES: WHY AFRICAN-AMERICAN MARRIAGES ARE IN CRISIS

He: My dear miss, de worl' is a howlin' wilderness full of devourin' animals, and you has got to walk through hit. Has you made up yer min' to walk through hit by yerself, or wid some bol' wahyer?[5]

In reply, the women needed to be skilled in responding to a series of riddled questions. In this way, she would facilitate the outcome of the wooing. A young admirer might say, "Good lady, ef I was to give you a handkerchief to wash n' iron, how would you do it widout water or iron?" If the lady wanted to initiate the success of her admirer, she would answer, "Iron it with love."[6]

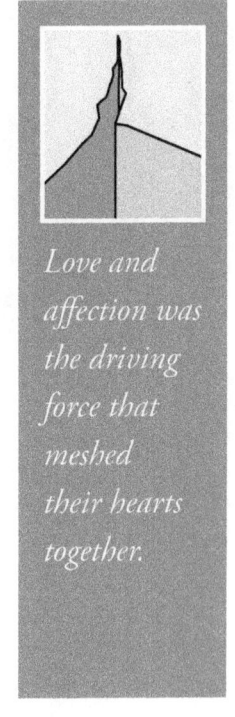

Love and affection was the driving force that meshed their hearts together.

Love and affection was the driving force that meshed their hearts together. As the slaves were given Saturday evenings off, many well-meaning gentlemen found their way to visit someone special. As the courtship developed into true love, the subject of marriage was sure to follow. In his 1849 narrative, Henry Bibb, an ex-slave, shares his days of falling in love and committing to marriage:

> "...on one Saturday evening. I called to see Malinda, at her Mother's residence, with an intention of letting her know my mind upon the subject of marriage. It was a very bright moonlight night; the dear girl was standing in the door, anxiously waiting my arrival. As I approached the door, she caught my hand with an affectionate smile, and bid me welcome to her mother's fireside.[7]

WHERE THE FAULT LIES: WHY AFRICAN-AMERICAN MARRIAGES ARE IN CRISIS

Some slaves were engaged for up to one year before marrying:

> ". . . on the Sunday evening following, I called on her again; she welcomed me with all the kindness of an affectionate lover, and seated me by her side. We soon broached the old subject of marriage, and entered upon a conditional contract of matrimony...that we would marry if our minds should not change within one year . . ."[8]

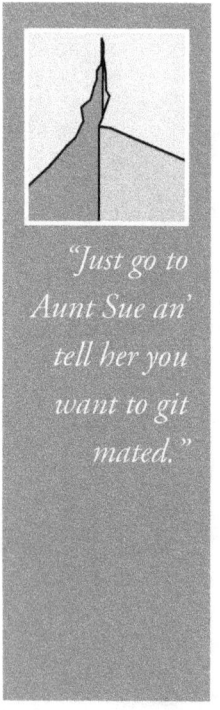

"*Just go to Aunt Sue an' tell her you want to git mated.*"

During the engagement period, the man would prepare a cabin and furniture for his family. The woman would start collecting items to establish her home.[9]

Some slaveholders allowed the slave community to regulate whether or not a wedding should take place. In one recount, the slaves did not have to ask the master: "Just go to Aunt Sue an' tell her you want to git mated. She tells us to think 'bout it hard fo' two days, cause marryin' was sacred in the eyes of Jesus."[10] Although slaves were not allowed to marry legally, they considered themselves married in the eyes of God, and even though many couples lived together without any formal ceremony, marriage was sacred and held with high regard. Whenever possible, they would go out of their way to formalize their unions:

> "When I was 21 years old I married. My husband worked on a farm a mile or so from the Fray place. In the south the slaves from two or three plantations live in a compound and when a couple marries they

just start living together without any ceremony. A ceremony wasn't much good for a slave wasn't allowed to take any vows. But I was really married. My husband and I went to another slave on his place who could read and write and knew something of the bible. I was proud of my marriage…and I sure got mad when anybody said anything about us, not being married."[11]

The slave community was determined to create their own ceremonies to acknowledge their commitments. Crossing large tree branches or sticks was one way that couples chose to show their commitment. This symbolized the vitality and tenacity of trees. Stepping high across a broomstick was another way they chose to show their commitment. When they jumped the broomstick, they were married. This feat was a humorous test to see who would rule the family.[12]

Other slave communities created marriage "by the blanket", and the couple would come together in the same cabin. The bride would bring her blanket and lay it down besides the groom; they were married! Many slaves desired to have a Black preacher perform the ceremony. The weddings of house slaves were quite elaborate. A White preacher would perform the ceremony and read from the Bible. The wedding would be attended by the slaveholder's family and invited guests. An elaborate dinner and dancing would add to the festive occasion.[13] Henry Bibb remembered clearly his special day.

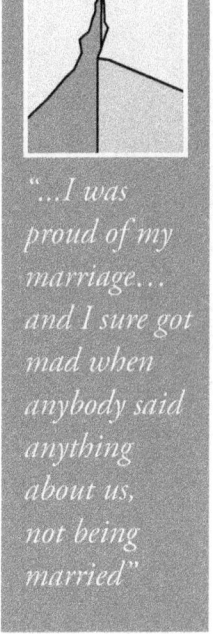

"…I was proud of my marriage… and I sure got mad when anybody said anything about us, not being married"

"All appeared to be wide awake, and we had quite a jolly time at my wedding party. And notwithstanding, our marriage was without license or sanction of law, we believed it to be honorable before God, and the bed undefiled. Our Christmas holydays were spent in matrimonial visiting among friends…I often look back to that period even now as one of the most happy seasons of my life…"[14]

The slaveholders reaction to slave marriages were mixed. Most slave owners conceded to allow marriage, but some refused to encourage it, and others flatly refused to allow it at all. Many slave owners were clearly disturbed with any proceedings, grand or otherwise that gave the slave express permission to experience life in a natural setting.

One slaveholder expressed his outrage in his daily writings:

Slaveholders preferred the couple to live on one plantation for security.

"Their mistress gave them a grand supper (which they did not deserve)…I did not wish to be here to see the tomfoolery that was going on about it, as if they were ladies of quality. They had out, with wife's permission of course, very foolishly, my crockery, tables, chairs, candlesticks, and I suppose everything else they wanted."[15]

This slaveholder was incensed that his slaves were pretending to be equal to White people. Slaveholders could not bare the thought that their slaves were on the same level as themselves.

Most slave owners strongly encouraged their slaves to marry because men who were married were less likely to plan to escape. Slaveholders preferred the couple to live on one plantation for security. In this way, the slave would have less reason to leave the plantation. They reasoned that a Black man who loved his wife and his children was less likely to rebel or to run away, than would a "single" slave.[16] Affluent masters frequently purchased the female slave to ensure the males loyalty. In any case, if the couple were allowed to marry and live on different plantations, it could be changed or revoked at anytime. Many husbands and wives did accomplish living on neighboring plantations. The slave would visit his wife about once a week. He would bring his soiled clothing and good things collected during the week home to his wife.[17]

Many slaves could not bear to see their wives mistreated, so they preferred a distal living arrangement. According to Henry Bibb:

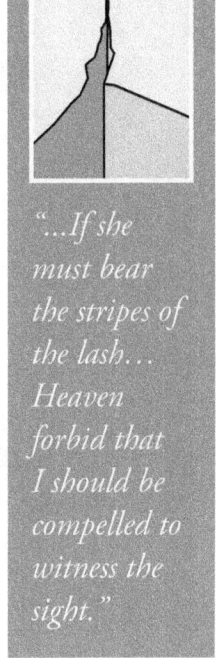

"...If she must bear the stripes of the lash... Heaven forbid that I should be compelled to witness the sight."

> "I was opposed to living with Malinda, who was then the centre and object of my affections—but to live where I must be eye witness to her insults, scourgings and abuses, such as are common to be inflicted upon slaves, was more than I could bear. If my wife must be exposed to the insults and licentious passions of wicked slave drivers and overseers; If she must bear the stripes of the lash…Heaven forbid that I should be compelled to witness the sight."[18]

Other slave narratives expressed the same sentiments as well. According to Moses Grandy, "No colored man wishes to live at the house where his wife lives, for he has to endure the continual misery of seeing her flogged and abused, without daring to say a word in her defense."[19] Slavery challenged the very essence of manhood. One researcher concluded that very

WHERE THE FAULT LIES: WHY AFRICAN-AMERICAN MARRIAGES ARE IN CRISIS

few men who loved a woman rarely escaped "wounded pride, enduring anger, and a diminished sense of manhood."[20]

Husbands who were allowed to live with their wives learned to suffer quietly as not to cause further harm to their families. Living on one plantation throughout a slave's lifetime would be considered an exception. More often than not, a slave would live on at least two or more plantations during his lifetime. Separate living arrangements became a by-product of slavery.[21]

Another consideration of the slave union included matrimony between a slave and a free Black. According to one county record, 47% of the free Blacks that married chose slave spouses.[22] Harriet Tubman, the famous Underground Railroad conductor, courted and married a free Black man in 1844. Her planned escape took place without her husband when she heard rumors of being sold with her brothers and sisters.[23]

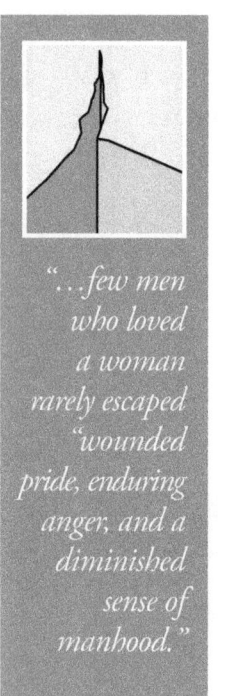

"...few men who loved a woman rarely escaped "wounded pride, enduring anger, and a diminished sense of manhood."

Many slaves longed for the opportunity to purchase freedom for their loved ones. Arrangements could be made for some slaves to purchase their mate. For example, a free Black carpenter in Maryland, named George Berry, reached an agreement with his wife's master that he would be allowed to purchase her within three years after their marriage for $750.00. Of course, this held some risk. Promises could and were often broken, and some were sold away. [24]

Although slaves who fell in love were willing to purchase one another, not all requests for this type of arrangement were granted. For example, in her 1861 narrative, Harriet Jacob feared that her master's affection toward her might destroy her chances at marrying the free man with whom she had fallen in love. After summoning her to his study, her master initiated the following conversation:

"So you want to be married, do you? said he, "and to a free...?"

"Yes, sir."

"Well, I'll soon convince you whether I am your master, or the... fellow you honor so highly. If you *must* have a husband, you may take up with one of my slaves."

What a situation I should be in, as the wife of one of his slaves, even if my heart had been interested!

I replied, "Don't you suppose, sir, that a slave can have some preference about marrying? Do you suppose that all men are alike to her?"[25]

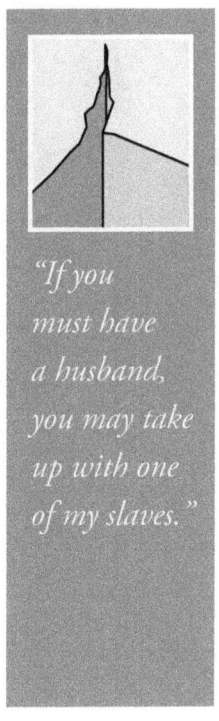

"*If you must have a husband, you may take up with one of my slaves.*"

The master was angered by her response and eventually punished her for even considering it. In the end, Harriet was denied the opportunity to be purchased by the man she loved and wanted to marry. Her conclusion to this experience led her to ask, "Why does the slave ever love?"[26] Since any decision to marry was subject to the whimsical temperament of the master, many slaves went to great lengths to guard their hearts from falling in love.

Others vowed never to marry while in the clutches of slavery. When asked if he had a family, the Rev. J. W. Loguen responded by saying, "I determined long ago never to marry until I was free. Slavery shall never own a wife or child of mine."[27] William Wells Brown wrote, "Getting married while in slavery was the last of my thoughts...I knew if I should have a wife, I should not be willing to leave her behind; and if I should attempt to bring her with me, the chances would be difficult for success."[28] If they did consider marriage before becoming free, it was restricted to certain conditions:

> "After having broached the subject of marriage, I informed her of the difficulties which I conceived to be in the way of our marriage; and that I could never engage myself to marry any girl only on certain conditions...I was religiously inclined; that I intended to try to comply with the requisitions of the gospel...Also that I was decided on becoming a free man before I died, and that I expected to get free by running away...Agreement on those two cardinal questions I made my test for marriage."[29]

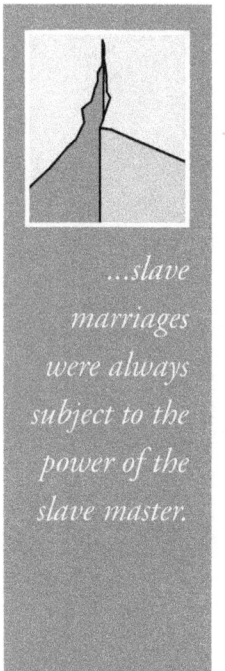

...slave marriages were always subject to the power of the slave master.

Since the possibility of being forced to leave loved ones had to be considered, liberty was one subject that had to be discussed before marrying.

Although couples continued to fall in love and commit to marriage, there is no doubt the lifestyle of aggression, abuse, and powerlessness, especially for men, filtered into their personal relationships. Several slave documents attest to marital spats, from verbal abuse to domestic violence. These altercations were rarely reported since some slave owners whipped their slaves for arguing or fighting. In any case, if slave couples were granted a divorce or were separated, in the end, slave marriages were always subject to the power of the slave master.[30]

QUESTIONS FOR REFLECTION AND DISCUSSION

1. As a *point of entry*, what are some of the issues mentioned that might be considered in understanding the nature of today's crisis?

2. How did the slave community compensate for the disregard held for their marriages?

3. In 1849, Henry Bibb declared, "I never will give my heart nor hand to any girl in marriage, until I first know her sentiments upon the all-important subjects of Religion and Liberty." The bible tells us to be equally yoked with our marriage partner. Why is this important?

*...So then, they are no longer two but one flesh. Therefore what God has joined together, **let no man separate.***
(Matthew 19:6, NKJV)

- III -
A SPIRITUAL ASSAULT: FORCED TERMINATION

Slave marriages were not secure during slavery. Whatever the form of marriage, a slave owner had the right to end the union. Forced termination was common. As noted earlier, a slave husband might be ordered to take another wife, or surrender his own wife for the night for the master's personal pleasure. In either case, the slave had no right to protest. Another way a slave husband might be separated from his wife was through slave sales. Slave owners sold their slaves for a variety of reasons. Since slaves were considered property, they were considered assets. If the owner found himself in debt personally or for business reasons, he could liquidate his debt by selling his slaves.[1]

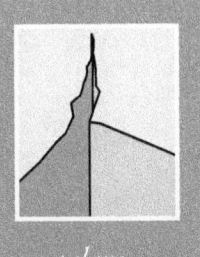

...a slave husband might be ordered to take another wife, or surrender his own wife for the night for the master's personal pleasure

" . . . a trader was seen talking to my master. The slaves were in a state of consternation, saying, 'Is it me? Is it me? Who'll go next?' One of the slaves said 'See, they are selling the pigs to go to Virginia. They don't seem to care, but we can't be like pigs, we can't help thinking about our wives and children.' The slaves were all taking their dinners in their cabins about two o'clock. My master, the trader, and three other White men walked up to the cabins, and entered one of them. My master pointed first to one, and then to another, and three were immediately handcuffed, and made to stand out in the yard. One of the slaves sold had a wife and five children on another plantation; another slave had a wife and three children; and the other had a wife and one child… My master said, "Take your pick of the women." The "trader" said, 'I'll give you 800 dollars for that one.' My master said, 'I'll take it.'"[2]

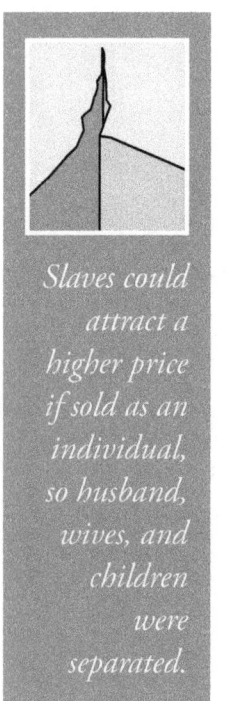

Slaves could attract a higher price if sold as an individual, so husband, wives, and children were separated.

The "traders" were in the official business of buying and selling slaves. They would serve as middlemen between the upper south and buyers in the lower south. These slave-trading companies generally bought their slaves off the auction block and sold them for profit in another state.[3] The breeding of slaves for sale became a specialized business. One such company, Price, Birch & Company were self-proclaimed "Dealers in slaves." This trading house held women, men, and children in guarded rooms. The prices ranged from $2,500 or $2,800 for a strong male, to $250 for a small child.[4]

Keeping a good public image was important to most slave-traders; therefore they refuted any claims that their selling practices netted the break-up of slave families. But according to auction records, this practice was the "rule rather than the exception in this business". Slaves could attract a higher price if sold as an individual, so husband, wives, and children were separated.[5]

The slaveholders' self-fulfilling purposes took precedence over any quest to keep families together. One reason for separating the slave family was the death of the master. Creditors would relentlessly force the sale-off of slaves for the payment of debts. Another reason was to maintain the lifestyle of the master's family.[6]

The practice of selling slaves left the heart of slave families entrenched in deep sorrow. "An auction was synonymous with breaking up of families. The most emotional scenes took place at the foot of the auction block."[7] The slaves could not bear the thought of being separated from their loved ones. Forced separation was considered the most traumatic event of slavery. Grown men were known to plead and cry to spare their loved ones. Mothers screamed and wrestled with masters only to be pushed aside. Others chose to fight the slave owner, overseer, and trader in vain. Many slaves, angry and overcome with grief never recovered. In his 1859 narrative, Charles Ball remembered his father's countenance after his wife was sold away from him:

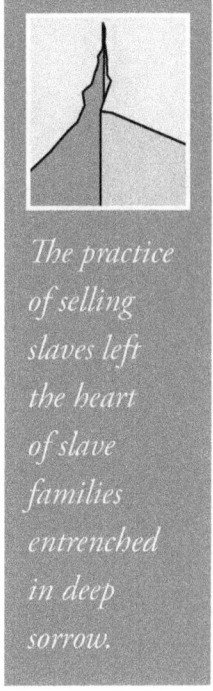

The practice of selling slaves left the heart of slave families entrenched in deep sorrow.

> "My father never recovered from the effects of the shock, which this sudden and overwhelming ruin of his family gave him. He had formerly been of a gay, social temper…After this time I never heard him laugh heartily, or sing a song. He became gloomy and morose in his temper, to all but me…"[8]

The shock of being separated caused many to go insane, have hallucinations, or even commit suicide. One woman who had been sold from her husband and children while being shipped on a boat to another port was so despondent that she jumped overboard and drowned herself.[9]

Charles Ball even recollected his thoughts of suicide after being torn from his family:

> "I had times serious thoughts of suicide, so great was my anguish. If I could have got a rope I should have hanged myself at Lancaster. The thought of my wife and children I had been torn from in Maryland, and the dreadful undefined future which was before me, came near driving me mad."[10]

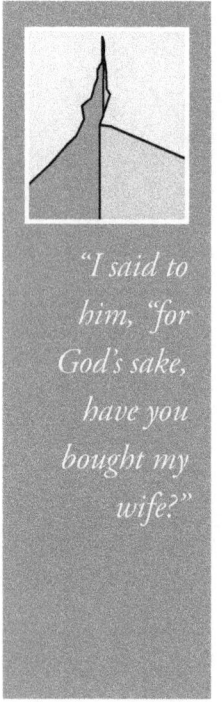

"I said to him, "for God's sake, have you bought my wife?"

Several ex-slave biographies solemnly reveal the anguish experienced as a result of this practice. Referring to another account of this tragedy:

> "I said to him, "for God's sake, have you bought my wife? He said he had; when I asked him what she had done; he said she had done nothing, but that her master wanted money. He drew out a pistol, and said that if I went near the wagon on which she was, he would shoot me. I asked for leave to shake hands with her, which he refused, but said I might stand at a distance and talk with her. My heart was so full, that I could say very little…I have never seen or heard of her from that day to this. I loved her as I love my life"[11]

In the narrative of Henry Box Brown, Brown describes the day when his wife and children were sent to the auction mart and sold:

"I cannot express, in language, what were my feelings on this occasion. I received a message, that if I wished to see my wife and children, and bid them the last farewell, I could do so, by taking my stand on the street...I stood in the midst of many who, like myself, were mourning the loss of friends and relations and had come there to obtain one parting look at those whose company they but a short time before had imagined they should always enjoy,..."[12]

Unfortunately, many slave marriages were commonly affected by this practice. A traumatic event like this could provoke a slave to run away.

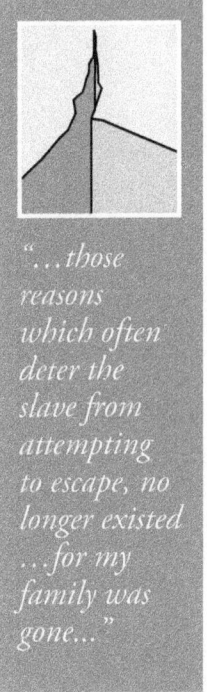

"...those reasons which often deter the slave from attempting to escape, no longer existed ...for my family was gone..."

"The first thing that occurred to me, after the cruel separation of my wife and children from me, and I had recovered my senses, so as to know how to act, was, thoughts of freeing myself from slavery's iron yoke. I had suffered enough under its heavy weight, and I determined I would endure it no longer; and those reasons which often deter the slave from attempting to escape, no longer existed... for my family was gone,..."[13]

Some couples were able to escape together before a forced separation could take place. In one article printed in the "Voice of the Fugitive" in 1851, Mr. John Moore describes a daring escape involving him and his wife. Mr. Moore initially escaped and fled into the state of Indiana. Once there, he worked and saved his wages for two months. At the end of this period, he returned to his former master, handed over his earnings, and explained that he was tired of freedom. He admitted that the abolitionists were not to be trusted and he was better off with a secure home. His master was moved by his honesty.

The master's neighboring friends were not so trusting. They suggested that he be sold. They believed he had only returned to steal his wife who lived on a neighboring plantation. The master was impressed with his slave's loyalty, so he refused his neighbor's advice. To avoid suspicion, the couple had a big argument and Mr. Moore refused to have anything to do with his wife. Secretly, he would meet her late at night.

> *Free Blacks in the North could be kidnapped from their families and sold south.*

As the wife's master became convinced that Mr. Moore was not a threat, he began to allow the wife out alone without watching her. One day she asked to leave on Saturday night with permission to stay until Sunday evening. This request was granted and in the end, John Moore, his wife, and two others arrived safely in Canada.[14]

Forced separation also touched the lives of free couples. Free Blacks in the North could be kidnapped from their families and sold south. One such case was the infamous kidnapping of Solomon Northup. Northup was a free man who lived in Saratoga N.Y. with his wife Anne, and three children. He was a talented fiddler, craftsman, and farmer.

In the spring of 1841, Northrup was approached by two strangers who offered him temporary employment. Thinking he would return soon with his wages, he left without saying goodbye to his family. The strangers drugged him and robbed him of his free papers. Shortly after waking from a drugged state, Northup tried to assert his authority as a free man, but to no avail. He was soon to realize his fate. He now belonged to another man who sold him to the slave trading Company of Price & Birch. Separated from his wife and children, he was now to live as a field hand in Louisiana for the next 12 years.

Northup never forgot his family and Mrs. Anne Northup never gave up hope. Northup managed to send a letter to friends in the North concerning his whereabouts. Mrs. Northup also petitioned the Governor of New York, which led to her husband's freedom in 1853.[15]

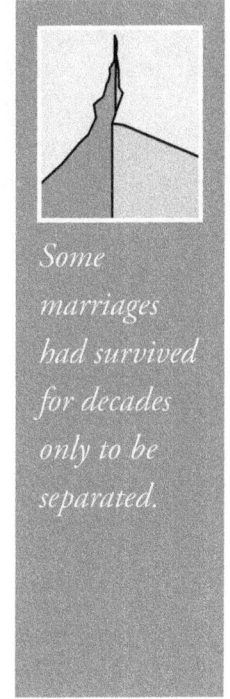

Some marriages had survived for decades only to be separated.

Many couples were separated early in their union, and others were separated after several years of marriage. Some marriages had survived for decades only to be separated. According to historian Herbert Gutman in the state of Mississippi:

> "One in four marriages registered in 1864-1865 involved one or two persons separated by force from a spouse in an earlier marriage. In marriages in which either partner was at least forty years old in 1864-1865, the percentage in which one or both spouses had experienced an earlier marriage that had been broken by force rose to 35 percent.

REASONS FOR THE BREAKUP OF EARLIER SLAVE MARRIAGES GIVEN IN 1864-1865 BY PERSONS REGISTERING MARRIAGES IN WHICH ONE OR BOTH PARTNERS WERE AT LEAST FORTY YEARS OLD, DAVIS BEND, NATCHEZ, AND VICKSBURG, MISSISSIPPI

Number of marriages registered in 1864-1865 in which one or both partners were at least forty years old	1910
Couples in 1864-1865 not reporting an earlier terminated marriage	29%
Couples in 1864-1865 reporting an earlier marriage terminated by mutual consent	4%
Couples in 1864-1865 reporting an earlier marriage terminated by desertion	5%
Couples in 1864-1865 reporting an earlier marriage terminated by force	35%
Couples in 1864-1865 reporting an earlier marriage terminated by death	41%

Note: *These percentages add up to more than 100 percent because in some instances persons registering marriages had more than one earlier marriage.*

Among people that old, seven in ten marriages registered in 1864-1865 included one or two people who had been married earlier. Nearly as many of these 1864-1865 marriages included a prior marriage broken by force as broken by death..."[16]

Southern churches were confronted with the ramifications of forced separation. The Clergy struggled with the idea of slaves wanting to remarry after the slave's mate had been sold. The church argued that forced separation of a married couple did not dissolve the marriage. On the other hand, many churches were sympathetic to the hardship and came to recognize forced separation equal to the death or divorce of a legal marriage.[17]

If left intact, many marriages lasted for decades; slave couples had a deep respect for marriage. Henry Bibb believed that "there are no class of people in the United States who so highly appreciate the legality of marriage, as those persons who have been held and treated as property."[18] Mr. Henry Box Brown also shared his sentiments about the sanctity of marriage:

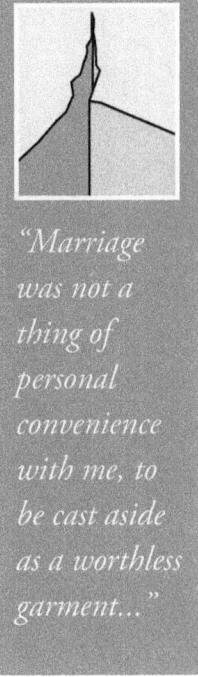

"Marriage was not a thing of personal convenience with me, to be cast aside as a worthless garment..."

> "It is true, as my master had told me, that I could "get another wife;" but no man, excepting a brute below the human species, would have proposed such a step to a person in my circumstances; and as I was not such a degraded being. I did not dream of so conducting. Marriage was not a thing of personal convenience with me, to be cast aside as a worthless garment, whenever the slaveholder's will required it: but it was a sacred institution binding upon me, as long as the God who had "joined us together," refrained from untying the nuptial knot."[19]

WHERE THE FAULT LIES: WHY AFRICAN-AMERICAN MARRIAGES ARE IN CRISIS

Many of the marriages broken by force dreamed of coming together again by Emancipation, but many slaves did remarry. Before the Civil War, Laura Spicer and her children were sold away from their husband and father. Mr. Spicer eventually remarried but continued to encourage his wife through letters to seek a new husband:

"I would much rather you would get married to some good man, for every time I gits a letter from you it tears me all to pieces. The reason why I have not written you before, in a long time, is because your letters disturbed me so very much. You know I love my children. I treats them good as a Father can treat his children; and I do a good deal of it for you. I am sorry to hear that Lewellyn, my poor little son, have had such bad health. I would come and see you but I know you could not bear it. I want to see you and I don't want to see you. I love you just as well as I did the last day I saw you, and it will not do for you and I to meet. I am married, and my wife have two children, and if you and I meets it would make a very dissatisfied family.

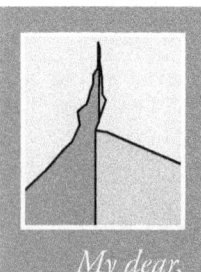

My dear, you know the Lord knows both our hearts. You know it never was our wishes to be separated...

Send me some of the children's hair in a separate paper with their names on the paper. Will you please git married, as long as I am married. My dear, you know the Lord knows both our hearts. You know it never was our wishes to be separated from each other, and it never was our fault. Oh, I can see you so plain, at any-time, I had rather anything to had happened to me most than ever to have been parted from you or Anna. If I was to die, today or tomorrow, I do not think I would die satisfied till you tell me you will try and marry some good, smart man that will take care of you and the children; and do it because you love me; and not because I think more of the wife I have got than I do of you.

The woman is not born that feels as near to me as you do. You feel this day like myself. Tell them they must remember they have a good father and one that cares for them and one that thinks about them every day—My heart did ache when reading your very kind and interesting letter. Laura I do not think I have change any at all since I saw you last—I thinks of you and my children every day of my life. Laura I do love you the same. My love to you never have failed. Laura truly, I have got another wife, and I am very sorry, that I am. You feels and seems to me as much like my dear loving wife, as you ever did Laura. You know my treatment to a wife and you know how I am about my children. You know I am one man that do love my children...."[20]

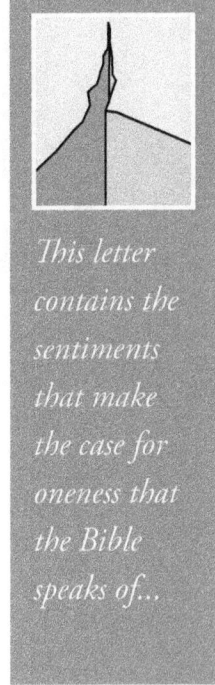

This letter contains the sentiments that make the case for oneness that the Bible speaks of...

This letter contains the sentiments that make the case for oneness that the Bible speaks of in Genesis 2:24, "*Therefore a man shall leave his father and mother and be joined to his wife, and they shall become one flesh.*" In the New Testament, Jesus is found reconfirming this same truth with a question to the Pharisees, *"Have you not read....For this reason a man shall leave his father and mother and be joined to his wife, and the two shall become one flesh?" (Matthew 19:4a, 5, NKJV)*

When the flesh is torn it hurts. Mr. Spicer finds himself longing for the wife that was torn from his side. Although he was living in harmony with his new wife and children, he could not forget his first family. There was a conflict between two laws, earthly and spiritual. Jesus speaks directly to this cause by saying, *"...Therefore what God has joined together, let no man separate" (Matthew 19:6b, NKJV).* Although, Southern law did not protect slave marriages, the Divine law was still in operation; therefore many spouses, by no fault of their own, could not help but feel genuinely torn. Forced termination was truly, and by all historical accounts, one of the greatest tragedies of the heart.

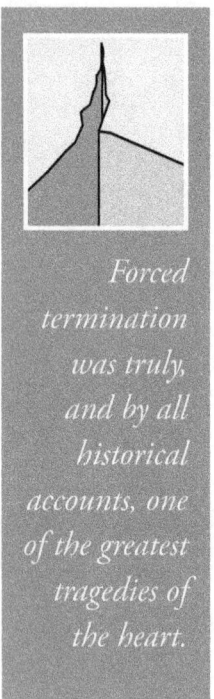

Forced termination was truly, and by all historical accounts, one of the greatest tragedies of the heart.

QUESTIONS FOR REFLECTION AND DISCUSSION

1. Are there any similarities between the forced termination of slavery and voluntary separation of African-American marriages today?

2. In light of the statements made by former slaves, Henry Bibb and Henry Box Brown, concerning their respect for marriage, what statement would you make today about the institution of marriage? What statements have you heard others making?

I have cried until the tears no longer come; my heart is broken, my spirit poured out, as I see what has happened to my people; little children and tiny babies are fainting and dying in the streets.
          (Lamentations 2:11, TLB)

~ IV ~
CAUGHT IN THE CROSSFIRE: GRIEVING WITH GOD FOR THE CHILDREN

*A*nother tragedy of slavery was the capture of African children from their families in Africa. As noted earlier, during a slave raid eleven-year-old Olaudauh Equiano was captured along with his younger sister only to be separated and forced into slavery. Thousands of young children suffered the same fate, but unlike Olaudauh, many died during the long journey to the Americas. Once in the United States, children born to African slaves inherited a lifetime of servitude. The legal status of a child born to an enslaved mother was identified with the status of the mother. In 1662, a Virginia law declared that "…all children born in this country shall be held bond or free only according to the condition of the mother." If the mothers became free after childbirth, the children belonged to the slaveholder.[1]

> "…all children born in this country shall be held bond or free only according to the condition of the mother."

Although the African tradition welcomed and honored having children, pregnancy was welcomed with mixed emotions. The ill fate of slavery and hopes of raising the family together drew a sense of fear and uncertainty. Slave couples wrestled with the thought of birthing a child into a lifetime of slavery. Slave narratives reveal the deep anguish they felt. In one slave narrative, Henry Bibb shares his perspective on being a father:

"...I could never look upon the dear child without being filled with sorrow and fearful apprehensions...If ever there was any one act of my life while a slave, that I have to lament over, it is that of being a father and a husband of slaves. I have the satisfaction of knowing that I am only the father of one slave. She is bone of my bone, and flesh of my flesh; poor unfortunate child. She was the first and shall be the last slave that ever I will father, for chains and slavery on this earth."²

One slave mother wrote:

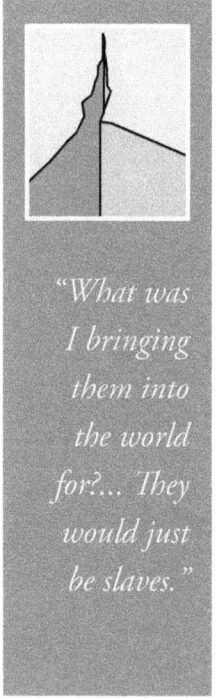

"What was I bringing them into the world for?... They would just be slaves."

"How well I remember how I would sit in my room with the little ones on my lap and the tears would roll down my cheeks as I would ponder the right and wrong of bringing them into the world. What was I bringing them into the world for? To be slaves and go from morning to night. They couldn't be educated and maybe they couldn't even live with their families. They would just be slaves. All that time I wasn't even living with my husband. He belonged to another man. He had to stay on his farm and I on mine."³

Heavy work schedules and couples living on two separate plantations excluded the presence of many slave fathers. The separation of husband and wife left the fate of a pregnancy in the hands of the slave-owner. Miscarriages, sterility, stillborns, and sudden-infant death plagued slave quarters. Prenatal care was non-existent, and the possibility of dying in childbirth followed each pregnancy. The high infant mortality rate was no doubt a direct link to poor nutrition and strenuous work. The care of slave women varied. Some slave owners decreased their workload and provided extra food. Others provided work in "trash gangs", which consisted of light agricultural work.[4] But many pregnant slaves received very little attention. There was a belief that slave women bore children "more easily and quickly than White women".[5]

Although special treatment was not given, the slave woman's womb was valued as an asset, and efforts were taken to avoid miscarriage. Up until the owners and overseers knew that the women were absolutely pregnant, they would continue to work them as usual. Treaty and Lousine, two women owned by the Georgia slaveholder John B. Lamar, suffered miscarriages in 1855. Lamar suspected that his overseer, Stancil Barwick, had been abusive to the two female slaves, but Barwick claimed that he was unaware of the pregnancies until the women had lost the fetuses.[6]

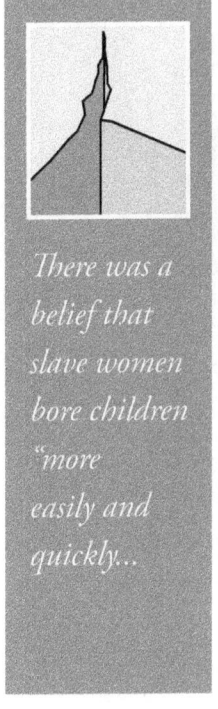

There was a belief that slave women bore children "more easily and quickly...

The slave owner was concerned with bringing his investment to full term, and another consideration taken in keeping the womb safe was in the execution of punishment. To punish a pregnant slave: "Dey [the White folks] would dig a hole in de ground just big 'nuff fo' her stomach, make her lie face down and whip her on de back to keep from hurtin' de child."[7] Sometimes slave women who had been whipped experienced complications during childbirth. The loss of a fetus was common due to various complications. If the newborn survived more than a few days, the child was given a name to honor a relative. Some slave owners changed the name of the children. If the slave parents were not pleased with the name, they would assert their authority by refusing to call them by the name in private. They would teach the child his given name only to be heard by his family members.[8]

Some slave mothers were sent back to the fields the next day, which hindered the bond between mother and child. Many mothers had to take their infants to the cotton fields, hoping to lay them in the shade or a safe place while they performed endless hours of labor. Many children died in the fields due to a lack of care. One slave husband blamed the death of his infant twins on his wife's inability to care for their children after receiving a vicious beating at the hands of his master and mistress. "I was trembling from head to foot, for I was powerless to do anything for her...My twin babies lived only six months after that, not having had the care they needed..."[9]

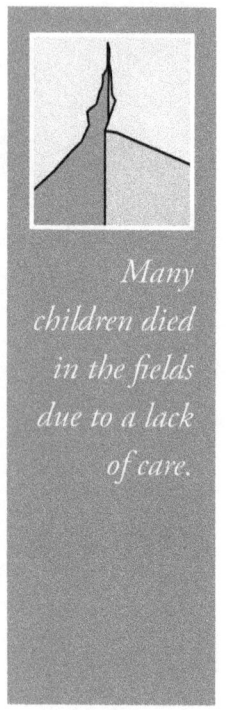

Many children died in the fields due to a lack of care.

On large plantations, once the mother returned to work, either an elderly slave or the slaveholder's wife cared for the babies. Although childhood as we know it was short lived, many slave narratives attest to young children playing games, hunting, and fishing. Soon the differences became apparent. Siblings as young as seven or eight years were caretakers if needed. Many children were given small chores by the age of four. While, most were working full-time between the ages of ten and twelve.[10]

Slave parents worked together when possible to provide for their children. Slave fathers worked long hours, and would go without necessities to provide for their wife and children. This required that some men would have to work on Sundays for neighboring planters to provide what was considered luxuries for the family. In his 1859 narrative, Charles Ball retells why his friend had no choice but to work on Sundays:

> "He said, that for several years past, he had not been able to provide any clothes for himself; as he had a wife with several small children, on an adjoining plantation, whose master gave only one suit of clothes in the year to the mother, and none of any kind to the children, which had compelled him to lay out all his savings in providing clothes for his family, and such little necessaries as were called for by his wife from time to time. He had not had a shoe on his foot for several years, but in winter made a kind of moccasin for himself of the bark of a tree…"[11]

"I remember, when a child, our parents used to tell us that we would not be always slaves."

Many slave parents taught their children how to pray and instilled the hope of a better day. In the slave narrative of John Quincy Adams, he attested to his religious upbringing and how his mother and father took him and his twenty-four siblings to church every Sunday. Mr. Adams remembered his mother's words of encouragement: "I remember, when a child, our parents used to tell us that we would not be always slaves. It made me feel glad to think that I would be free someday or other."[12] Although parents tried to buffer the effects of slavery on them by tenderly loving their children and instilling hope, they could offer no protection from an abusive owner. Parents taught their children how to avoid punishment at a very early age. Some children were just infants or toddlers and too young to understand the implications of their crying or curious behavior.

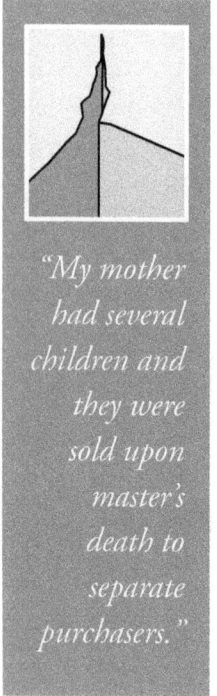

"My mother had several children and they were sold upon master's death to separate purchasers."

"Little Frances was a pretty child; she was quiet, playful, bright and interesting...She was left at the house to creep under the feet of an unmerciful old mistress, whom I have known to slap with her hand the face of little Frances, for crying after her Mother, until her little face was left black and blue.... Who can imagine what could be the feelings of a father and mother, when looking upon their infant child...But we were all claimed and held as property; the father and mother were slaves!"[13]

The separation of children from their parents was yet another harsh reality of being a slave parent. Many adult slaves vividly remembered being taken as children. Charles Ball also never forgot being torn from his mother's arms at the age of four.

"My mother had several children and they were sold upon master's death to separate purchasers. She was sold, my father told me, to a Georgia trader. I, of all her children, was the only one left in Maryland. When sold I was naked, never having had on clothes in my life, but my new master gave me a child's frock, belonging to one of his children. After he had purchased me, he dressed me in this garment, took me before him on his horse, and started home; but my poor mother, when she saw me leaving her for the last time, ran after me, took me down from the horse, clasped me in her arms, and wept loudly and bitterly over me... My master seemed to pity her; and endeavored to soothe her distress by telling her that he would be a good master to me...the slave driver, who had first bought her, came running in pursuit of her with a rawhide in his hand. When he overtook us, he told her he was her master now...My mother then turned to him and cried, "Oh master, do not take me from my child!" Without making any reply, he gave her two or three heavy blows on the shoulders with his raw-hide, snatched me from her arms...the cries of my poor parent became more and more indistinct – at length they died away in the distance, and I never again heard the voice of my poor mother."[14]

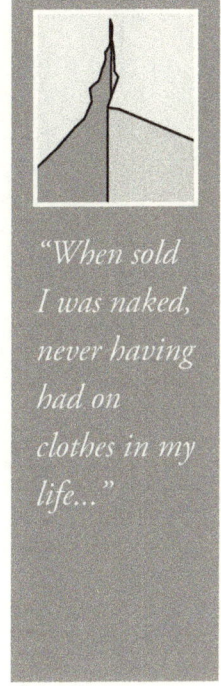

"When sold I was naked, never having had on clothes in my life..."

Charles was sold again at age twelve to another owner who he described as treating him poorly. At about the age of twenty he was hired out for a year, only to be eventually sold again. Except this time, he met and married a woman named Judah. Horribly, shortly after establishing his own family, he was sold again and shipped to another state away from his wife and children.[15] In all this, Charles Ball reached adulthood from being sold as a child, got married, and started his own family only to experience the same grief with his own offspring. In turn, his children had the same story to tell as they had suffered the same loss. From one generation to the next, forced separation continued to affect the entire family.

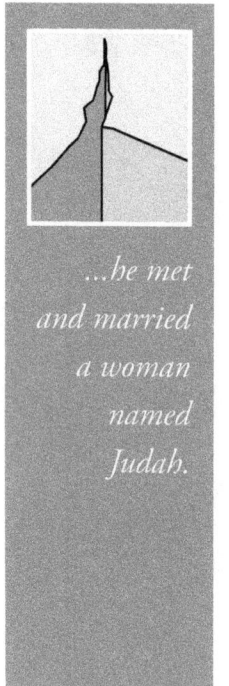

...he met and married a woman named Judah.

QUESTIONS FOR REFLECTION AND DISCUSSION

1. What fears are African-American children experiencing in the 21st century? What fears are parents facing?

2. How was the absent father during slavery different from the absentee father of today? How is he similar?

Listen to my prayer, O God; Do not ignore my cry for help! Please listen and answer me, for I am overwhelmed by my troubles,...My heart is in anguish. The terror of death overpowers me, Fear and trembling overwhelm me. I can't stop shaking. Oh how I wish I had wings like a dove; then I would fly away and rest! I would fly far away to the quiet of the wilderness. How quickly I would escape—far away from this wild storm of hatred...
(Psalm 55:1, 2, 4-8, TLB)

- V -
PSYCHOLOGICAL WARFARE: THE PSYCHOLOGICAL EFFECTS ON WOMANHOOD AND MANHOOD

The slave's spirituality and the family unit certainly preserved the minds of many slaves. Yet, psychologically, it was a constant battle because of the cruel and unusual punishment. Fear was the primary weapon of oppression. It was the mitigating force that kept the slaves from uprisings and attempts to run away. From the fear of being separated from your family, to the fear of the lash, fear was the primary weapon used to influence the opinions, emotions, attitudes, and behavior of the slave.

Fear was the primary weapon of oppression.

Parents tried to mentally prepare their children for the harshness of slavery. Children were taught at an early age about obedience and the "driver's lash". At age 17, Frederick Douglass was sent to a slave-breaker because he was not obedient to his master. He was considered troublesome and unruly. Six months under the slave-breaker caused him eventually to be broken, he says, in "body, soul, and spirit". Extreme cruelty was used to strip away the slaves will for resistance and independence. Frederick Douglass wrote about his stay under this slave-breaker:

"I shall never be able to narrate the mental experience through which it was my lot to pass during my stay at Covey's...I suffered bodily as well as mentally...The over work, and the brutal chastisement of which I was the victim, combined with that ever-gnawing and soul-devouring thought—"I am a slave—a slave for life...a living embodiment of mental and physical wretchedness."[1]

...there was a limit to the amount of cruelty slaveholders wanted to inflict on their "said" property.

Slave women were subject to the same type of abuse, in addition to constant sexual exploitation. One woman who was carrying a baby failed to run fast enough to reach the overseer's house for roll call. She was disrobed and given twelve lashes for her lateness. Whatever the charge, women were also submitted to the cruelty of the lash.[2] But there was a limit to the amount of cruelty slaveholders wanted to inflict on their "said" property. The life of a slave was worth much more to the slave owner. He wanted loyal obedient slaves.

Since this was the case, an environment conducive to maintaining control was put into place. The use of verbal aggression was one of the techniques used to maintain control. Slaves were constantly called out of their given names with vulgarities that degraded the men and humiliated the women. Solomon Northup was introduced to this fact after being kidnapped:

"Reading from his paper, he called, "Platt". No one answered. The name was called again and again, but still there was no reply. Then Lethe was called, then Eliza, then Harry, until the list was finished, each one stepping forward as his or her name was called.

"Captain, where's Platt?" demanded Theophilus Freeman. The captain was unable to inform him no one being on board answering to that name.

"Who shipped *that* nigger?" he again inquired of the captain, pointing to me.

"Burch," replied the captain.

Your name is Platt—you answer my description.

"Why don't you come forward?" he demanded of me, in an angry tone.

I informed him that was not my name; that I had never been called by it, but that I had no objection to it as I knew of.

"Well, I will learn you your name," said he, "and so you won't forget it either, by—," he added."[3]

He was not only subjected to being called out of his name, but even experienced the powerlessness of having someone change his name. In this instance, a man who had only known the image of being a free man now has to submit to the image set forth for him by his captors.

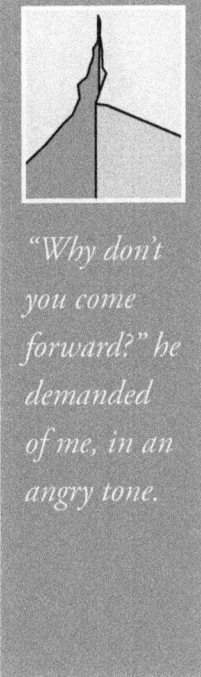

"Why don't you come forward?" he demanded of me, in an angry tone.

The misinterpretation of scripture was another way slave owners tried to accomplish control. The Bible was used to support the claims that having black skin was a curse, along with the belief that God did not see everyone as equal. Both of these claims were an attempt to invoke a sense of shame toward Blackness, and bolster the superiority of Whiteness. To support these claims a false doctrine was preached. As a confession of faith, slaves learned to repeat false doctrine in hopes of creating the desired servant. An excerpt from a Catechism published in 1862 illustrates the procedure:

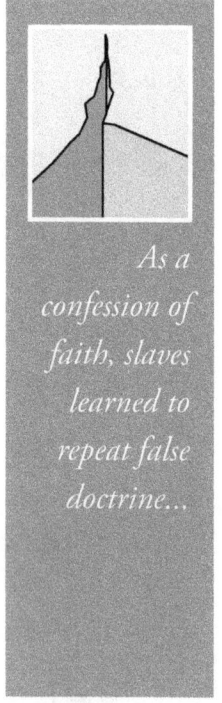

As a confession of faith, slaves learned to repeat false doctrine...

Q. How are you to show your love to [your master and mistress] and your parents?
A. I am never to lie to them, to steal from them, nor speak bad words about them; but always to do as they bid me.
Q. But can you not disobey your parents [and your master] without their knowing it?
A. Yes; but God knows it; for God always sees me.
Q. You promised, you say, to keep the commandments;—How must you feel towards God and man, in order rightly to keep them?
A. I must "love God with all my heart; and my neighbor as myself."
Q. Who is your neighbor?
A. Every body who lives with me, and around me, and has the control over me.
Q. Can you name some persons?
A. My playfellows, [my master and mistress] and my parents.[4]

WHERE THE FAULT LIES: WHY AFRICAN-AMERICAN MARRIAGES ARE IN CRISIS

Some slaves took this doctrine to heart. There were loyal obedient Christian slaves who commanded a fair price if ever sold. According to several slave narratives, many slaves never fully accepted this doctrine in a true sense. They knew they had to obey the master for survival, but they also believed in a God who delivered the oppressed. They identified with the Israelites of the Old Testament and began to sing and pray for their deliverance.[5]

Lastly, because the slaveholder had economic reasons to naturally increase his slaves, he also attempted to control the family unit by redefining it. Slave women were counted as mothers, and the men as laborers. For the overseer, the complete nuclear family was not necessary. As mentioned earlier, slaves preferred to live on separate plantations from their spouses, but not all for good reasons. Some slaves on neighboring plantations were involved in bigamous relationships. This behavior was well known and encouraged by the slaveholder. The more children the slaves could produce, the greater the slaveholder's financial worth.[6] Therefore, the African-American man was defined by his physical strength and his ability to produce children.

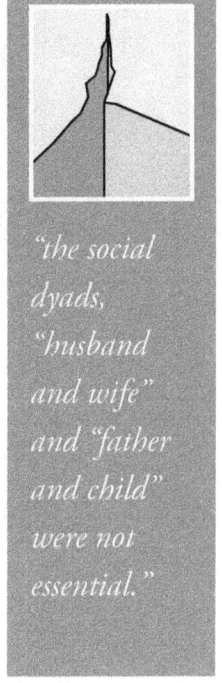
"the social dyads, "husband and wife" and "father and child" were not essential."

Slave women were defined by their ability to be an effective breeder. Slave women who could not bare children were sold. Again, the slave woman's offspring was not considered a burden, but an asset to the owner. Many owners viewed the slave woman as a mother, and not as a wife. Children were thus conceived out of convenience for the system. According to historian Herbert Gutman, in the reproduction of slaves, "the social dyads, "husband and wife" and "father and child" were not essential."[7] Thus, through this entire process the nature of the family unit was systematically violated.

QUESTIONS FOR REFLECTION AND DISCUSSION

1. What spiritual seeds of conflict were planted during slavery?

2. Concerning the seeds you identify——In what ways can the fruit of these seeds be seen today?

So the people believed; and when they heard that the Lord had visited the children of Israel and that He had looked on their affliction, then they bowed their heads and worshiped.
    (Exodus 4:31, NKJV)

~ VI ~
SAFE HOUSES:
"SPIRITUAL SONGS"

Like the "safe houses" of the Underground Railroad, the family provided shelter that kept the slaves from becoming consumed by the slaveholder's authority. In the absence of parents who were sold away, extended kinships would become the child's aunt or uncle. The family provided empathetic understanding and familial support. In this way, the family and the slave community became an important buffer for the trauma experienced during slavery. Ultimately, for many families, their greatest source of strength came from their spirituality.

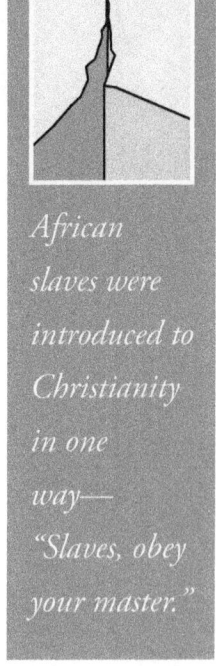

African slaves were introduced to Christianity in one way—"Slaves, obey your master."

African slaves were introduced to Christianity in one way—"Slaves, obey your master."[1] The missionary plan was to create an ideal master-slave relationship. They believed Christianity would soothe the tension between slaves and masters. Plantation missionaries urged slave owners to apply Christian beliefs in their relationship to the slave. Ministers constantly reminded owners of their duty to the slave: To provide for them, care for them in old age, and protect them from abuse. On the other hand, they never went as far as to question the authority of the slaveholder. A frequently taught scripture was Colossians 4:1, *"Masters, give unto your servants that which is just and equal; knowing that ye also have a Master in heaven." (KJV)* [2]

WHERE THE FAULT LIES: WHY AFRICAN-AMERICAN MARRIAGES ARE IN CRISIS

One of the reasons many slaves were spared cruel treatment was due to the religious beliefs of their slaveholders. Henry Bibb wrote about a Christian owner who ascribed to his beliefs:

> "I once knew a Methodist in the state of Ky., by the name of Young, who was the owner of a large number of slaves, many of whom belonged to the same church with their master. They worshipped together in the same church. Mr. Young never was known to flog one of his slaves or sell one. He fed and clothed them well, and never over worked them. He allowed each family a small house to themselves with a little garden spot, whereon to raise their own vegetables..."[3]

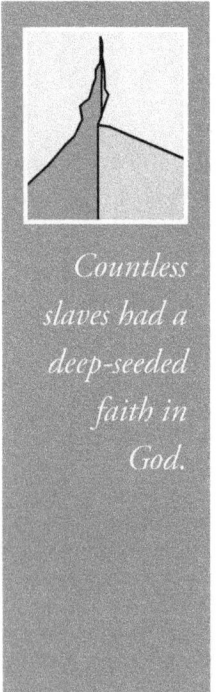

Countless slaves had a deep-seeded faith in God.

Even religious slave owners were careful not to give their slaves too much freedom. They thought that allowing Christianity in the slave society would spark rebelliousness. Many owners of slaves even forbid them to pray or to practice religion.

Some slave owners allowed their slaves to pray and worship because they assumed that religion would keep the slaves in the position of submissiveness. This assumption was not true because many African-American slaves took Christianity seriously. Countless slaves had a deep-seeded faith in God. They believed the slaveholder to be the sinner and began to pray for deliverance. They identified with the Israelites as God's chosen people and believed God would deliver his people out of bondage.

To gather for comfort, the slaves would have private religious meetings in the night. They would announce the gathering by singing, "Steal Away To Jesus." One slave recounts: "The masters before and after freedom didn't like them religious meetings, so us naturally slips off at night, down in the bottom of somewheres. Sometimes us sing and pray all night."[4] For the slave, the church was not a building, but a group of believers congregating with a common purpose. The "meetings" would provide a place for fellowship, song, and praise. It provided an outlet for free expression of the spirit, away from the watchful eye of the "master".

The slave song throughout all historical accounts was an integral part of the worship experience. All who heard them described the slave spirituals as unique creations. "When Baptist Negroes attended the church of their masters...they used hymn books, but in their own meeting they often made up their own words and tunes. They said their songs had more religion than those in the books."[5]

For the slave, the church was not a building, but a group of believers congregating with a common purpose.

The explanation of making up words and tunes (spontaneous songs), are without doubt expressions of the "spiritual songs" mentioned in scripture. Apostle Paul's writing to the church of Ephesus admonished them to, *"be filled with the Spirit; speaking to yourselves in psalms and hymns and **spiritual songs**, singing and making melody in your heart to the Lord" (Ephesians 5:18-19).* "The Greek word is 'ode pneumatikos, meaning songs of the pneuma—the breath of God."[6] The book of Psalms is full of spiritually inspired singing that lamented to God. In Psalm 142, we find David crying out to God.

> *I cry out to the Lord with my voice; With my voice the Lord I make my supplication. I pour out my complaint before Him; I declare before Him my trouble. When my Spirit was overwhelmed within me, Then You knew my path...I cried out to You, O Lord: I said "You are my refuge, My portion in the land of the living. Attend to my cry. For I am brought very low; Deliver me from my persecutors, For they are stronger than I. Bring my soul out of prison, That I may praise Your name...*
> *(Psalm 142: 1-3, 5-7, NKJV)*

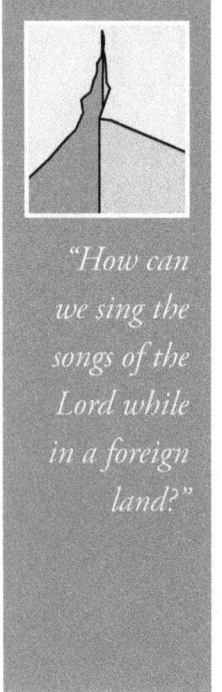

"How can we sing the songs of the Lord while in a foreign land?"

The "cry" was the sentiment of several songs found in the Psalms. For example, *"How can we sing the songs of the Lord while in a foreign land?" (Psalm 137:4, NIV)*. Of this scripture, LaMar Boschman comments, "Captivity had cost these people their songs of joy so that they had nothing left but songs of supplication and lamentation."[7]

Captivity certainly cost Africans their songs of joy that they sang on the shores of Africa. Their songs turned into songs of lamentation and supplication as they longed to be free. The song of the slave Frederick Douglass wrote expressed "The sorrows of the heart."[8] Slave songs also recounted historical facts for all to remember. For example, as slaves were carried away they often sang these words:

> "See these poor souls from Africa
> Transported to America;
> We are stolen, and sold in Georgia,
> Will you go along with me?

> We are stolen, and sold in Georgia,
> Come sound the Jubilee!
> See wives and husbands sold apart,
> Their children's screams will break my heart;—
> There's a better day a coming,
> Will you go along with me?
> There's a better day a coming,
> Go sound the jubilee!" [9]

As the slave song developed into a unique sound, so did their praise meeting. Unlike the congregational Sunday morning meeting with their masters, the slave community conducted their meetings with dancing, song, and praise. One such song was:

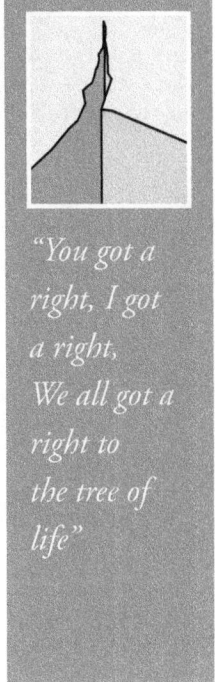

"You got a right, I got a right, We all got a right to the tree of life"

> "You got a right, I got a right,
> We all got a right to
> the tree of life;
> Yes, you got a right, I got a right,
> We all got a right to
> the tree of life.
> The very time I thought I was los'
> The dungeon shook
> an' the chain fell off.
> You may hinder me here
> But you cannot there
> 'Cause God in his heaven
> Goin' to answer prayer.
> O Brethren, You got a right.
> I got a right
> We all got a right to
> the tree of life."[10]

The contents of this song would only be sung at the praise meetings found in the backwoods. The slave holding community would have been uncomfortable with such a declaration of rights on a Sunday morning. On the other hand, for the slave community, this song of declaration sung in an expressive praise may have ended in an outburst of being filled with the Holy Ghost (Spirit).

The music was the sound of their soul. Singing in communion with God allowed them to pour out their troubles and to look to Him to supply all their needs. Whether sung aloud or in secret, they looked to God's power to break the evils of slavery.

Once the box was opened, Mr. Brown released a new song...

"O, gracious Lord! When shall it be,
That we poor souls shall be free;
Lord, break them slavery powers —
Will you go along with me?
Lord break them slavery powers,
Go sound the jubilee!

Dear Lord, dear Lord, when slavery'll cease,
Then we poor souls will have our peace—
There's a better day a coming.
Will you go along with me?
There's a better day a coming,
Go sound the jubilee!"[11]

Many "spirituals" revealed a desire to be delivered from bondage. But they also included lyrics that captured hope for a brighter day. That day certainly came for the famous Henry Box Brown when he reached freedom after mailing himself to an abolitionist in a box. Once the box was opened, Mr. Brown released a *new song* from his spirit. In his quest to give thanks, notice that he sang from the Psalms to give praise and adoration to the Deliverer!

"I waited patiently, I waited patiently for the Lord, for the Lord, And he inclined unto me, and heard my calling;
I waited patiently, I waited patiently for the Lord,
    And he inclined unto me, and heard my calling
    And he hath put a new song in my mouth,
Ev'n a thanksgiving, Ev'n a thanksgiving,
    Ev'n a thanksgiving unto our God
Blessed, Blessed, Blessed, Blessed, is the man,
    Blessed is the man,
Blessed is the man that hath set his hope, his hope in the Lord;
    O Lord my God, Great, Great, Great,
    Great are the wondrous works which thou hast done, which thou hast done,
    Great are the wondrous works,
    Great are the wondrous works, which thou hast done.
    If I should declare them and speak of them, they should be more, more, more than I am able to express.
    I have not kept back thy loving kindness and truth from the great congregation,
    I have not kept back thy loving kindness and truth from the great congregation..." [12]

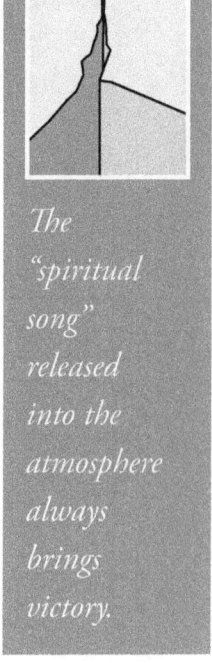

The "spiritual song" released into the atmosphere always brings victory.

The *"spiritual song"* released into the atmosphere always brings victory. By the 1730s, the Evangelicals condemned slaveholding as a sin. Their theology consisted of sanctification, spiritual rebirth, and evangelism. "Truly born-again Christians, they taught, will know through the Spirit to free their slaves and evangelize them." The Biblical arguments continued in the United States. By 1845 the Presbyterians, Methodists, and Baptists inspired great controversy that spawned the Civil War. The abolitionists of the North and the proslavery people of the South used the Bible to prove their points. The Civil War finally resolved the conflict.[13]

QUESTIONS FOR REFLECTION AND DISCUSSION

1. How was the spiritual song like a "safe house" for the slave? How is the spiritual song or prophetic song a "safe house" for us today?

2. The strength of the spirit was evident in their resiliency to survive slavery. What can we do to help strengthen the spirits of our brothers and sisters who appear weary of their marriages?

Singing from the Psalms:
Henry Box Brown sang his own rendition of Psalm 40. God hears and loves our personal praise. Read through this excerpt from Psalm 96, then begin to make melody with the words making it your own song of praise!

> *Oh sing to the Lord a new song!*
> *Sing to the Lord, all the earth.*
> *Sing to the Lord, bless His name;*
> *Proclaim the good news of His salvation from day to day.*
> *Declare His glory among the nations,*
> *His wonders among all peoples.*
> *For the Lord is great and greatly to*
> *be praised…(Psalm 96:1-4, NKJV)*

Persecuted, but not forsaken, cast down but not destroyed.
　　　　(II Corinthians, 4:9, KJV)

THE END OF SLAVERY

*R*eading about the enslavement of African-Americans or any group of people can be painful. Before moving on to the next section, to bring forth closure, be alert to any pain from past offenses that need to be healed. Share with the Lord in your own way about how you feel, or pray the ending prayer below. Spiritual soldiers cannot fight effectively if they are wounded.

A Prayer:

Heavenly Father, my heart is saddened when I think of the time of wilderness for my brothers and sisters of African descent. But I trust in You Lord, with all my heart, and lean not to my own understanding. It is because of Your Word, I take comfort in knowing that You were there. Thank You for showing them the secret place (Psalm 91), where they found refuge through periods of grief and sorrow. Thank You for setting Your love upon them, and for sending the angels to take charge over them. For You are a loving God, full of mercy and truth. As I have considered the days of the past, I recognize Your strength in an adaptive and resilient people. So today, I surrender my pain unto You, that I might also exhibit the strength and tenacity of Your Spirit in times of distress and discomfort. As You minister to my heart, I thank You for replacing the pain with Your love and showering me with Your loving thoughts. For surely You have delivered us!

    Amen
    References: Psalm 91:1 & 11; 40:5

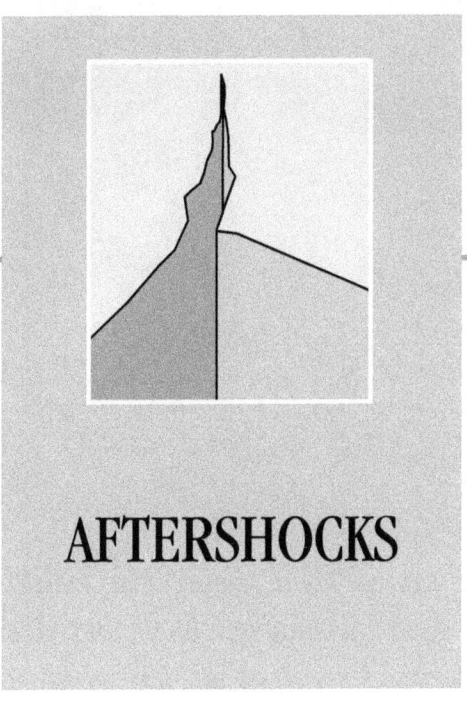

AFTERSHOCKS

PART II

The widespread custom of two centuries has not disappeared in forty years. Between three and four percent of the families are today separated, others have been and are remarried, usually without the trouble of a divorce, while others will separate in the future.

W.E.B. DuBOIS, AFRICAN AMERICAN SCHOLAR—1908

The law is good, then. The trouble is not with the law but with me...I don't understand myself at all, for I really want to do what is right, but I don't do it. Instead I do the very thing I hate.
 (Romans 7:14, 15, NLT)

THE IMPACT OF SLAVERY ON TODAY'S COUPLE

*A*fter Emancipation, couples tried to adjust to their new freedom. Unfortunately, African-American couples had to survive the riveting aftershocks of overt racism, lynching, and unemployment. By the 1900s, African-Americans migrated to the North in search of better opportunities for their families. Although the North brought some economic stability, similar hardships followed the husband and wife well into the 20th century.

Social scientists and psychologists have long debated the significance of slavery and its long-term affects. In their books, many African-American scholars such as William E. B. DuBois in 1908, and E. Franklin Frazier in 1939, believed that slavery weakened the family.[1] But later, contemporary critics suggested racism and joblessness were the culprits. Some social scientists believe that slavery happened too long ago to have any impact on contemporary behavior. Some revisionists believed that slavery had barely hurt families at all. But there are some scholars who remain convinced that the roots of the present-day difficulties of African-American relationships are embedded in slavery.[2]

African-Americans have made enormous progress and many couples have enjoyed stable loving relationships.

Certainly, African-Americans have made enormous progress and many couples have enjoyed stable loving relationships. However, there is still more work to be done. There is little question that the unnatural patterns of behavior that were forced upon slave couples have, in turn, taken on new forms. Forced separation has evolved into voluntary separation, leaving many children not knowing their true fathers. Curses spoken over the male and female have turned to curses spoken to each other, and the violence that was used to maintain human possession has filtered its way down into many current relationships. In all this, many African-American couples have unknowingly enforced the very thing that they have vehemently despised about the abuses of slavery.

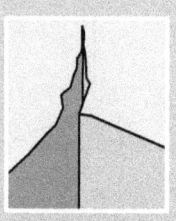

Hurtful patterns visibly rooted in the evils of slavery must be discerned and rooted out!

Recognizing historical patterns that adversely affect the marital relationship is paramount when interceding for the African-American marriage. Hurtful patterns visibly rooted in the evils of slavery must be discerned and rooted out! So, in this section, we will look at how some of the remaining stereotypes that grew out of slavery can hinder the marital relationship. Then, we can move forward in not only understanding where the *fault* lies, but where the *solution* begins.

Don't copy the behavior and customs of this world, but let God transform you into a new person by changing the way you think. Then you will know what God wants you to do, and you will know how good and pleasing and perfect his will really is.
(Romans 12:2, NLT)

- VII -
BROKEN IMAGES: STEREOTYPES THAT DESTROY ONENESS

*A*frican-Americans were enslaved for over 300 years in response to negative stereotypes. This type of labeling in any instance—for any group of people—can lead to disaster. Many of us would stand guilty as charged if we were asked if we had ever been involved in stereotyping. This is why we must ask God, to cleanse our hearts and minds daily that we may not fall prey to *grouping* anyone negatively. It is important that we understand that having negative mindsets will only cause problems in our lives and in our relationships.

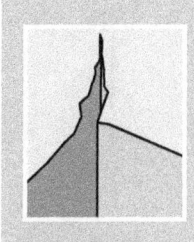

Negative stereotypes carry a powerful charge over its intended group.

What happens when negative stereotypes enter into the marital relationship? To answer this question, we must understand how we internalize and perceive stereotypes. The internalization of a stereotype can be simply stated as reading the script and acting out the part. On the other hand, perceiving a stereotype will cause one to judge the other person by the script. In either case, submitting to stereotypes can set the relationship up for failure. Therefore, understanding the impact stereotypes have on a relationship is important.[1]

Negative stereotypes carry a powerful charge over its intended group. One way this can be seen is when a person identifies with the negative portrayal of his group or culture. When something is sufficiently modeled, it can begin to shape what we believe about ourselves. Therefore, we become what we think. Proverbs 23:7 says, "*As a man thinketh in his heart, so is he...*" This classic scripture explains why some people give place to or accept negative behavior as their own. Stereotypes where men are characterized as unreliable, violent, and exploitative, and women as evil, suspecting, and domineering, set the stage for marital trouble.

If a husband or wife begins to mirror one of these negative character traits, it will become a major source of tension in the marriage. We can see this concept clearly illustrated in I Samuel chapter 25, where a husband lives out the negative character of his name.

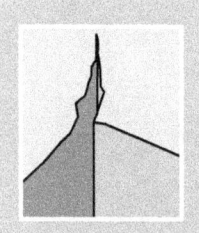

"Nabal...a Calebite, was surly and mean in his dealings."

*(3) His name was **Nabal** and his wife's name was Abigail. She was an intelligent and beautiful woman, but her husband, a Calebite, **was surly and mean in his dealings**. (4) While David was in the desert, he heard that Nabal was shearing sheep. (5) So he sent ten young men and said to them, "Go up to Nabal at Carmel and greet him in my name. (6) Say to him: 'Long life to you! Good health to you and your household! And good health to all that is yours!*

(7) "'Now I hear that it is sheep-shearing time. When your shepherds were with us, we did not mistreat them, and the whole time they were at Carmel nothing of theirs was missing. (8) Ask your own servants and they will tell you. Therefore be favorable toward my young men, since we

come at a festive time. Please give your servants and your son David whatever you can find for them.'"
(9) When David's men arrived, they gave Nabal this message in David's name. Then they waited.
(10) Nabal answered David's servants, "Who is this David? Who is this son of Jesse? Many servants are breaking away from their masters these days. (11) Why should I take my bread and water, and the meat I have slaughtered for my shearers, and give it to men coming from who knows where?"
(12) David's men turned around and went back. When they arrived, they reported every word.
(13) David said to his men, "Put on your swords!" So they put on their swords, and David put on his. About four hundred men went up with David, while two hundred stayed with the supplies.
(14) One of the servants told Nabal's wife Abigail: "David sent messengers from the desert to give our master his greetings, but he hurled insults at them. (15) Yet these men were very good to us. They did not mistreat us, and the whole time we were out in the fields near them nothing was missing. (16) Night and day they were a wall around us all the time we were herding our sheep near them. (17) Now think it over and see what you can do, because disaster is hanging over our master and his whole household. **He is such a wicked man that no one can talk to him.**"

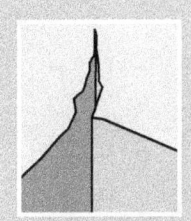

David said to his men, "Put on your swords!"

(18) Abigail lost no time. She took two hundred loaves of bread, two skins of wine, five dressed sheep, five seahs of roasted grain, a hundred cakes of raisins and two hundred cakes of pressed figs, and loaded them on donkeys. (19) Then she told her servants,

"Go on ahead; I'll follow you." But she did not tell her husband Nabal.
(20) As she came riding her donkey into a mountain ravine, there were David and his men descending toward her, and she met them. (21) David had just said, "It's been useless—all my watching over this fellow's property in the desert so that nothing of his was missing. He has paid me back evil for good. (22) May God deal with David, be it ever so severely, if by morning I leave alive one male of all who belong to him!"
(23) When Abigail saw David, she quickly got off her donkey and bowed down before David with her face to the ground. (24) She fell at his feet and said: "My lord, let the blame be on me alone. Please let your servant speak to you; hear what your servant has to say. (25) May my lord pay no attention to that wicked man **Nabal. He is just like his name—his name is Fool, and folly goes with him.** But as for me, your servant, I did not see the men my master sent...
(35) Then David accepted from her hand what she had brought him and said, "Go home in peace. I have heard your words and granted your request."
(36) When Abigail went to Nabal, he was in the house holding a banquet like that of a king. He was in high spirits and very drunk. So she told him nothing until daybreak. (37) Then in the morning, when Nabal was sober, his wife told him all these things, and his heart failed him and he became like a stone. (38) About ten days later, the LORD struck Nabal and he died. (I Samuel 25: 3-25, 35-38, NIV)

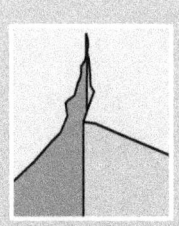

"She fell at his feet and said: "My lord, let the blame be on me alone."

This story is an example of the problems created when we image negative behavior. It will affect the entire family. Because of Nabal's unwitting behavior, David set out to kill every man under Nabal's authority. In this same way, the enemy wants to destroy our seed. Satan's strategy is for us to be ignorant of his devices, unknowingly giving him permission to operate in our lives. In this way, we would continue to walk in darkness, reading a script that was written for our destruction. False images of the past would then become set beliefs, carrying destructive thinking from one generation to the next.

To save future generations, interceding for the family is important, even when it is not our own that is being affected. Abigail was not responsible for her husband's behavior, but her intercession and humility saved the entire camp. Abigail waited until her husband was sober to tell him everything that had happened. With this news, his heart failed him and he later died. Prayerfully, as we become aware of the destruction involved in internalizing unhealthy ways, we will humble ourselves and allow God to put to death those things that hinder our relationships.

The perception of a stereotype can be just as damaging to a marriage as internalizing one.

The perception of a stereotype can be just as damaging to a marriage as internalizing one. In other words, the perception may not be the reality. We find this to be true in an episode found in II Samuel chapter 6, where David is confronted by his wife Micah, after she sees her husband dancing in the streets:

> *(16) Now as the ark of the Lord came into the City of David, Michal, Saul's daughter, looked through a window and saw king David leaping and whirling*

before the Lord; and she despised him in her heart.
(17) So they brought the ark of the LORD, and set it in its place in the midst of the tabernacle that David had erected for it. Then David offered burnt offerings and peace offerings before the LORD.
(18) And when David had finished offering burnt offerings and peace offerings, he blessed the people in the name of the LORD of hosts.
(19) Then he distributed among all the people, among the whole multitude of Israel, both the women and the men, to everyone a loaf of bread, a piece of meat, and a cake of raisins. So all the people departed, everyone to his house.
(20) Then David returned to bless his household. And Michal the daughter of Saul came out to meet David, and said "How glorious was the king of Isreal today. Uncovering himself today in the eyes of the maids of his servants, **as one of the base fellows shamelessly uncovers himself!***
(II Samuel 6:16-20, NKJV)

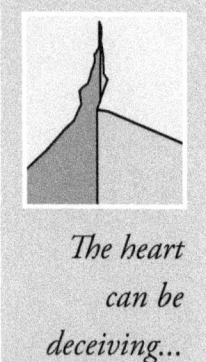

The heart can be deceiving...

Although King David was on his way to bless his own household after joyously blessing others, Michal surely felt that her husband's behavior was unbecoming of a king. She even went so far as to compare her husband with "*one of the base fellows*" who "*shamelessly uncovers himself*". Negative comparisons are never healthy for a marriage. The Bible also tells us she despised him in her heart. Here is that *heart* again. The heart can be deceiving, we may not readily admit or even be aware that we hold preconceived notions, but they can filter into our expectations of each other. For example, if a wife assumes that, for the most part, African-American men are unfaithful, she may burden her *faithful* and loving husband with false accusations. On the other hand, a husband who assumes all African-American women are domineering may strain his marriage with being overpowering and controlling towards a woman who understands her role as a wife. In both instances, this communication problem can create undue stress for the marriage.

In the end, the distorted messages received between couples that come from internalizing or perceiving negative stereotypes, can cause an onslaught of in-fighting where the stereotypes are no longer placed upon us, but become ammunition for the fight. Whatever the conflict between couples today—this type of distorted communication only confuses the real issue. Many African-American couples desire to have good relationships, but in order to send and receive the right messages, husbands and wives must first submit to the right image.

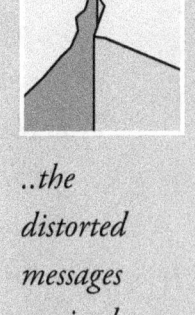

..the distorted messages received between couples... can cause an onslaught of in-fighting...

....put off, concerning your former conduct, the old man which grows corrupt according to the deceitful lusts, and be renewed in the spirit of your mind, and that you put on the new man which was created according to God, in true righteousness and holiness.
(Ephesians 4:22-24, NKJV)

- VIII -
OPTING FOR FREEDOM: A WORD ON DELIVERANCE

In 1863, the Emancipation Proclamation granted freedom to slaves in any state held by the Confederacy. As a tactic of war—the plan was to free slaves held in states in rebellion against the United States. Even though, at the time it was issued it could not be enforced, it would encourage slaves to flee their plantations—leaving the South stripped of labor needed to support the Confederate Army. Hundreds of thousands of slaves reached Union lines. But some slaves stayed with what they knew and fought alongside their masters. Due to conflicting information, other slaves were uncertain about their new status. Many questioned if they were really free.

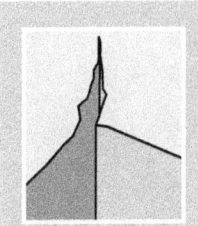

Broken images of the past have created too many lies...

Through this natural example, we can begin to make spiritual application in winning the war for our marriages. Since the plan is to win, God is encouraging us to walk away from those things that continue to hold us captive. We must desire to live in truth. Unlike the conflicting word surrounding the emancipation of the slaves, there is no conflict in the Word of God. Freedom for the African-American marriage *has* to be based on truth. Broken images of the past have created too many lies, which have masked our true identity. Therefore, gaining victory in our marriages has to start with knowing who we are in Christ. Otherwise, we become slaves to what we know, living beneath the privilege of our freedom.

To improve communication, we must be willing to exchange the enemy's lies with God's truth. This requires that we allow God to renew our minds. Then we can be free indeed! For the Word of the Lord says, *"If ye continue in my word, then are ye my disciples indeed; and ye shall know the truth, and the truth shall make you free." (John 8: 31&32, KJV)*

Walking in freedom also means that we must discipline ourselves to stand firm against any sin that has been passed down through preceding generations. We can see where this happened in II Kings 21 and 22, where two generations of Kings did evil in the sight of the Lord.

To improve communication, we must be willing to exchange the enemy's lies with God's truth.

Manasseh *was twelve years old when he became king, and he reigned fifty-five years in Jerusalem...And he **did evil in the sight of the Lord**...For he rebuilt the high places which Hezekiah his father had destroyed... (2 Kings 21:1-3, NKJV)*

Although, King Manasseh had a change of heart in his later years (2 Chronicles 33:12), his son Amon preferred to follow his father's earlier days.

Amon *was twenty-two years old when he became king, and he reigned two years in Jerusalem...And he **did evil in the sight of the Lord**, as his father Manasseh had done. So he walked in all the ways that his father had walked; and he served the idols that his father had served, and worshipped them. He forsook the Lord God of his fathers, and did not walk in the way of the Lord. (II Kings 21: 19-22, NKJV)*

One might assume that Amon's son might have internalized his father's sinful lifestyle, as Amon did his father's, but his son *chose* something different.

> *Josiah was eight years old when he became king, and he reigned thirty-one years in Jerusalem...And he **did what was right in the sight of the Lord**, and walked in all the ways of his father David; he did not turn aside to the right hand or to the left. (2 Kings 22:1, NKJV)*

Little Josiah chose to walk in the ways of God following King David, his father through heritage. Since families were big on sharing family lineage and history, perhaps someone had told him the ways of his father, King David. Like King Josiah, we too must decide to stop the cycles of negative behavior by sharing the heritage of our own families. And we too must make sure our children know the heritage of many of our African-American forefathers who received Christ, and were committed to the ways of God.

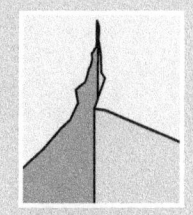

...perhaps someone had told him the ways of his father...

The Bible tells us that we overcome by the word of our testimony. If God has done anything for your marriage—tell another couple. Your testimony may be the life giving word needed to help them overcome their situation.

In conclusion, breaking patterns that hinder the marital relationship must be a committed work. However, don't worry, you won't have to go this one alone. God will never ask you to do anything He is not willing to empower you to do. For Philippians 4:13 says, *"for I can do everything God asks me to with the help of Christ who gives me the strength and power" (TLB)*. Surely, as we walk in His power, restoration miracles will be released all over the land.

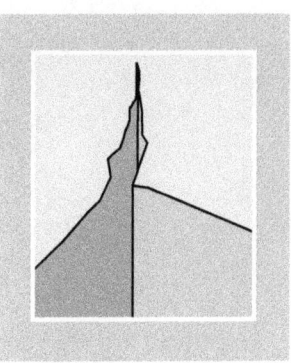

RESTORING THE FOUNDATION

PART III

Your miracle is not only found in your mind, but in your mouth. This is the season of family harvest!

APOSTLE H. DANIEL WILSON, SENIOR PASTOR 2004.

Then the Lord put forth his hand, and touched my mouth. And the Lord said unto me, Behold, I have put my words in thy mouth. See, I have this day set thee over the nations and over the kingdoms, to root out, and to pull down, and to destroy, and to throw down, to build, and to plant.
(Jeremiah 1:9-10, KJV)

A PROPHETIC PROCLAMATION

The Emancipation Proclamation released into the atmosphere was the turning point in winning a losing battle. It provided the catalyst needed to strengthen the fight. Winning the battle for our marriages not only requires us to turn from our old life, but to speak life. *"You will also declare a thing, And it will be established for you; So light will shine on your ways"* (Job 22:28, NKJV).

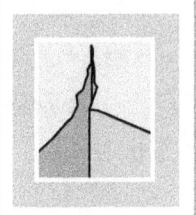

The husband and wife must be set free in the 21st century. The emancipation provided physical freedom, but spiritual freedom can only come through Christ. Commit to the Lord, and declare spiritual freedom for the African-American marriage.

> *Winning the battle for our marriages not only requires us to turn from our old life, but to speak life.*

A Prophetic Proclamation

In the name of Jesus, I speak now—to declare the decree of freedom over the 21st century marriage.
I call forth the plan of God, for marriages to be sealed in oneness.
I call wayward marriages back and declare them one flesh.
I declare marriages healed, restored, and revived.
I declare that the bond of oneness will restore every broken foundation.
I command that every evil thought or plan against marriages be brought into captivity to the obedience of Christ.
Father God, I thank You, for making me in Your image and Your likeness.
Therefore, I renounce all false images or destructive attitudes whose roots are founded in slavery and that hinder the body of Christ
in developing healthy relationships.
I declare the image of Christ in every marriage.
I loose the power of love, unity, and agreement, and call every marriage into covenant relationship.
I call marriages fruitful. Your children shall be an inheritance unto God as He has declared in His word. And you shall leave an inheritance to your children's children.
I call for marriage to prosper in integrity, intimacy, admiration, stability,
dependability, sensitivity, and accountability to God's Word.
I call the African-American household blessed.
Thank You, Lord for victory in marriage!

This is my commandment, That ye love one another, as I have loved you. Greater love hath no man than this, that a man lay down his life for his friends.
   (John 15:12 & 13, KJV)

- IX -
A SPIRIT OF REFORM: LEARNING TO LOVE GOD'S WAY

Reformers were agents for change that ignited various movements, from the anti-slavery movement to the civil-rights movement. God always has a plan and the people to reform the systems that go against His will for the Earth. As we release the declaration of faith and love over our families, we will release the power of God to reform marriages on the Earth. As we join the *MOVEMENT* of God—marriages will be set free! As we boycott behavior that hinders having healthy relationships, we will see the wall of divorce crumble under God's mighty hand.

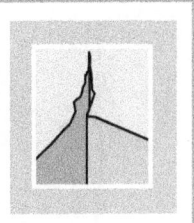

God is looking for couples who will submit to His leadership.

God is looking for couples who will submit to His leadership. Spirit guided relationships can stand the test of time. Remember earlier we looked at how the slave community practiced words of adoration and praise to win a mate, and amazingly throughout all of their human suffering they still found the right way to communicate their love for one another. God is calling us back to this type of love, the type of love that will ward off the current stressors of our time, and the type of love that will begin to build a fortress for the family.

Building a fortress starts with having the right idea about love. Today, love has become a mixed-up term with various meanings;

it could mean almost anything, depending on whom you talk to. Creative writers have tried to explain it, singers have tried to sing it, and movies have tried to portray it! And with all this going on, depending on what type of writing you read, what type of songs you sing, and what type of movies you like to watch, we could all be heading in the wrong direction. This is why we must learn to take our instructions on the subject of love, not from the latest video or the latest romance book, but from the Word of God.

Learning to love God's way is the only way to succeed in a covenant designed by God. How many of us have really considered the special instructions given to the husband concerning **love** in Ephesians 5:25-27?

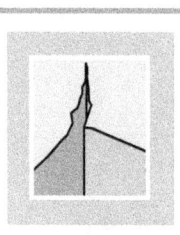

"...cleanse her with the washing of water by the word..."

*(25) Husbands, **love** your wives, just as Christ also loved the church and gave Himself for it, (26) that He might sanctify and cleanse her **with the washing of water by the word**, (27) that He might present her to Himself a glorious church, not having spot or wrinkle or any such thing, but that it should be holy and without blemish. (NKJV)*

In Song of Solomon, chapter 4:1-7, we find a passage of scripture that describes the passionate way a husband can communicate his love to his mate.

(1) Behold, you are fair, my love!
Behold, you are fair!
You have dove's eyes behind your veil.
Your hair is like a flock of goats,
Going down from Mount Gilead.

(2) *Your teeth are like a flock of shorn sheep.*
Which have come up from the washing,
Every one of which bears twins,
And none is barren among them.

(3) *Your lips are like a strand of scarlet,*
And your mouth is lovely.
Your temples behind your veil
Are like a piece of pomegranate.

(4) *Your neck is like the tower of David,*
Built for an armory,
On which hang a thousand bucklers,
All shields of mighty men.

(5) *Your two breasts are like two fawns,*
Twins of a gazelle,
Which feed among the lilies.

(6) *Until the day breaks, And the shadows flee away,*
I will go my way to the mountain of myrrh
And to the hill of frankincense.

(7) *You are all fair, my love,*
And there is no spot in you. (NKJV)

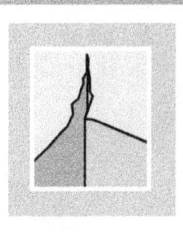

The Bible tells us that our tongues have the power to speak life or death in the Earth.

This is an example of the love language Christ expresses to His church. This type of love is powerful. The Bible tells us that our tongues have the *power* to speak life or death in the Earth. Proverbs 18:20-21 says, *"A man's stomach shall be satisfied from the fruit of his mouth; From the produce of his lips he shall be filled. Death and life are in the power of the tongue, And those who love it will eat its fruit."* As husbands impart words inspired by the Holy Spirit, the life giving words will prove to be the answer for many weary marriages.

While taking a lesson from the Song of Solomon, let us consider the role of a Godly husband as we keep in mind the instructions given in *Ephesians 5:26*. We can see that Solomon spoke words that caressed her soul. Verbal love, so to speak! Notice that Solomon greeted his bride by acknowledging her awe-inspiring beauty. Taking into account her *every* detail, he started with her eyes:

"*...You have dove eyes...*" he said.

Since our society is fast paced, husbands must remember to take the time to gaze into the eyes of their mate. The eyes share a type of communication that words sometimes cannot express. I am quite sure the Shulamite saw the Love of God in Solomon's eyes when he talked to her. Recognizing the *dove* or Holy Spirit that resides in the life of ones mate is also important. Having the right perspective will allow a husband to receive his wife as the helpmeet she is designed to be. Sometimes the wife can see things that the husband cannot see. Remember, although Noah was put in charge of the helm, he sent out the dove to see if there was dry land!

Traditionally, the bride wears a veil until the commitment, or covenant for oneness has been made.

"*You have dove's eyes **behind your veil***," he continued.

As Solomon gazed into her eyes, he could see how beautiful they were behind her veil. Behind something, you really cannot see straight through. Traditionally, the bride wears a veil until the commitment, or covenant for oneness has been made. Unfortunately, in some marriages, the wife wears an emotional veil because she does not feel the safety that comes with commitment and oneness. Sometimes this will happen if past issues have not been resolved, or when there has been a breech of trust in the relationship.

But here is the example of Christ: Solomon recognized the veil, but still looked through it! He was not hindered by what appeared to be between them. He was ready to be one with his bride. So, he opened his mouth and poured out God's Love–and started to wash her with God's selective Words:

"Your hair is like a flock of goats, Going down from Mount Gilead. "Your teeth are like a flock of shorn sheep, which have come up from the washing, Everyone of which bears twins, —and none is barren among them."

Men should let their wives know that they still notice their smile and the little things about them that make them unique. Just as human teeth need to be washed daily, words of adoration and praise need to be poured over a woman every day. If this is not done, the marriage will eventually decay.

Use the next verse as an example in letting a wife know what her words mean to you. *"Your lips are like a strand of scarlet, and your mouth is lovely."*

Men must let their wives know when they are found to be a Proverbs 31 woman. Commending a wife for her choice of words will let her know that what she has spoken into your life has influenced it in a great way. Many men fail to realize that constantly bringing attention to the negative without acknowledging the positive will only fuel negativity. When her words make you feel like a king, let her know.

Now watch this! The beginning of the next sentence says:

"Your temples behind your veil are like a piece of pomegranate."

Notice that after all this pouring and affirming, a wife may still have on a veil. At this point in the text, we must stop to think about why this might happen.

> *...you just can't get behind the veil. You must enter each court properly...*

WHERE THE FAULT LIES: WHY AFRICAN-AMERICAN MARRIAGES ARE IN CRISIS

Well, you just can't get behind the veil. You must enter each court properly with adoration and praise. Behind the veil is where Christ has blessed mankind with the ability to produce seed, to be fruitful in the Earth. It is an intimate place to become one, as a couple experiences the fruit of commitment. Intimacy between Christ and His Church requires that we approach Him with worship and praise to enter into His presence. So it also is with husband and wife. Because the man and woman are designed differently, wanting to get to the inner court without pouring out adoration in the outer court will eventually cause frustration in the marriage for both parties.

As marriages are reformed, couples will have to practice saying, more than parroting, common expressions—I love you—I love you too! God is calling couples to a higher place in Him, rather than to vain repetitions! Solomon could have just summed up his entire speech with, "I love you honey; you look nice today," but he had so much more to say:

"Your neck is like the tower of David, Built for an armory, on which hang a thousands bucklers, All shields of mighty men."

Men of God should not only openly admire their wives physical features, but acknowledge her as a tower of strength as well. We know that the *neck* supports the *head*. We must not misinterpret the definition of the statement that the wife is the weaker vessel, by making it mean that she is a weak vessel. She should be appreciated for the spiritual strength she brings to the relationship. Women have been known to travail in prayer for the men in their lives, and to shield them from the fiery darts of the enemy.

"Your two breasts are like two fawns, Twins of a gazelle, which feed among the lilies."

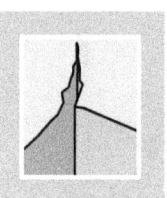

Behind the veil is where Christ has blessed mankind with the ability to produce seed...

Here, Solomon is talking to the Shulamite like the woman she is. He recognized that she was a mature woman deserving of the same respect as a mature man. God never meant for a man to have dominion over another person. *"Then God said, Let us make man in Our image, according to Our likeness; let **them** have dominion over the fish of the sea, over the birds of the air, and over the cattle, over all the earth and over every creeping thing that creeps on the earth" (Genesis 1:26, NKJV).* God has given men the HONOR to be the head of the household, leading his family with the love of Christ.

Now, how long is Solomon going to pour out his verbal love? So how long should a husband have to pour? The next verse tells us:

*"**Until** the **day breaks** and the shadows flee away..."*

The key word here is *until*. Husbands must be willing to wait until daybreak—they must be willing to pour and pour with their verbal love until something breaks and the shadows cast by the veil are torn away.

I John 4:18 says, *"There is no fear in love, but perfect love casts out fear, because fear involves torment But he who fears has not been made perfect in love."*

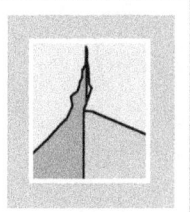

God never meant for a man to have dominion over another person.

See, Solomon wanted to be in oneness with his bride—the veil gets in the way.

Husbands must not let the veil of disappointment, hurt, rejection, or negative images get in the way of the love God wants to deposit in marriages today. One should allow the Holy Spirit to take control. He knows just what every individual marriage needs.

Once the *daybreaks*—joy will certainly come.

Next, he said, *"I will go my way to the mountain of myrrh and to the hill of frankincense."*

Letting a spouse know how far you will go to find something nice will keep the fire lit. Going to the mountains was no small feat, plus myrrh and frankincense were very special spices.

Now remember, order is the key in the Bible. Verse six is in the right position. In verses one through five, *words* are used to impart life and love. Through Christ, a husband can speak *words* that are inspired by the Holy Spirit, which have the power to break off any barriers between them. Then he can look for a special gift to top off the celebration!

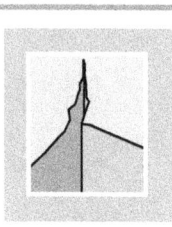

When we are submitted to the Holy Spirit, we can live out Galatians 5:22 & 23...

Lastly, Solomon says, *"You are all fair, my love, and there is no spot in you."*

Back in verse one, Solomon said, *"you are fair,"* and the word *all* is omitted.

Now we can get a better understanding of the scripture text in Ephesians 5:25-27. Men of God must submit to do the washing, so that *she* can be presented to her husband without spot or blemish, and without fault.

Once the spots are gone, oneness can begin. Verse nine says,

"You have ravished my heart, my sister, my spouse..."

They are not only married, but he called her his sister. Here is the oneness of the same parent—The Lord Jesus Christ.

Now, this is an example of the same love Christ shows the church. When we are submitted to the Holy Spirit, we can live out Galatians 5:22 & 23, *"But the fruit of the Spirit is love, joy, peace, patience, kindness, goodness, faithfulness, gentleness and self-control"* (NIV). If we look at the revelation that God is trying to show us through the Song of Solomon, chapter 4, we can see where each characteristic can be demonstrated.

For *love*—Respond to the love of God in your mates eyes.

For *joy*—Celebrate the victories in your marriage.

For *peace*—Recognize when you are being esteemed and honored.

For *patience*—Be willing to pour your verbal love until *daybreak*, taking care of the vessel that God entrusted you with.

For *kindness*—Never point out her flaws, even if she asks you to!

For *goodness*—Deal with her soul and spirit—tell her how beautiful she is, along with recognizing who she is in the spirit.

For *faithfulness*—Be willing to go that extra mile to make things special.

For *gentleness*—Use words that are soothing and supportive.

For *self-control*—Focus in on the positive.

Since, *"No one has seen God at any time. If we love one another, God abides in us, and His love has been perfected in us. By this we know that we abide in Him, and He in us, because He has given us of His Spirit." (1 John 4:12&13, NKJV)*

So get excited and join the *MOVEMENT*, and learn to love God's way!

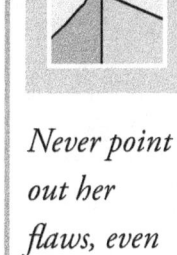

Never point out her flaws, even if she asks you to!

My Soul Mate

My prayers were answered on the day you and I met,
   I was totally speechless but my heart knew just what to say.
   I couldn't go off and try to hide myself from you,
   I couldn't hide my feelings from you any longer,
      I was now found by you.
   I knew that you were the one that my Lord sent to me,
      Through many trials and silent tears,
My prayers were answered with you.
                My Soul Mate

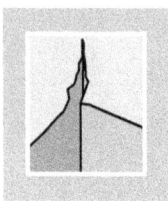

"I get so caught up in the moment... Spiritually, physically, mentally, and emotionally."

You really love the Lord my soul mate and it shows,
   Your love and kindness is more valuable than emeralds and sapphires,
      Just looking at you brings me joy.
   You are a rare treasure in God's treasure chest,
      A treasure that I will cherish and love with all my heart.
Each moment that we spend together is very precious,
   Every second, minute, and hour means so much to me.
At times I get so caught up in the moment,
   Wanting to show all my love for you.
Spiritually, physically, mentally, and emotionally.
   But I know that patience is the key in our relationship,
      O Lord what You have joined together let no man separate us,
      My prayers were answered with you,
         My Soul Mate

Vision with me my soul mate as time stands still,
   Where the sounds of nature echoes throughout the earth,
      Producing a harmonious melody of love and joy.

Where each note of I love you is played on the chords of our hearts,
　　The warm sun-rays of the sun outline your silhouette,
　　　　Up against the golden brown mountains of the Grand Canyon.
　　As your chocolate skin mingles with the sun-rays
　　　　Sparks of fire works fill the sky.
　　The sweet fragrances of roses fills the circumference of the universe,
　　　　Silent whispers of love is echoed through space and time
　　　　Into the souls of our hearts.
　　Voices of an angelic choir sing praises to our God.

O my feelings inside for you is like a chocolate waterfall,
　　Flowing down stream along the shores of your heart.

Let me look at you my soul mate as we walk side-by-side,
　　Through an emerald garden of love,
　　　　Let me hold your hand,
　　　　Let me look into your eyes,
　　　　Let me touch your lips with mine.

As your crystal tears run gently down your face,
　　You stand speechless,
　　　　Your heart is filled with peace,
　　　　Your mind is at ease,
　　　　　　and your soul has been comforted with love,
　　Heaven rejoices as we come together as one,
　　　　For your beauty is captured on the canvas of my heart.

　　　　My prayers were answered with you.
　　　　　　My Soul Mate

O my feelings inside for you is like a chocolate waterfall...

My Soul Mate, by Brian Lee Copyright© 1996. Used by permission.

If we do what helps them, we will build them up in the Lord...
        (Romans 15:2, NLT)

- X -
BUILDING SAFE HOUSES: MENTORING AFRICAN-AMERICAN COUPLES

*O*nce the fault line is created (like history), it can never be erased. But, seismologists use the information learned from history to save future lives. Likewise, ministry leaders, intercessory teams, Christian counselors, and individuals alike must be aware of the areas that play a part in sabotaging African-American marriages. For African-American couples, if marital tension is centered near the "historical" fault line discussed earlier (possibly through stereotype behaviors), the marriage designed for oneness will be more likely to disrupt.

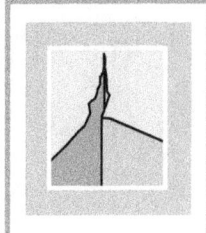

As an Apostolic Church, we must plant comprehensive marriage ministries...

Since an Earthquake may occur on the same fault line, we must be willing to create "safe houses" for the children in our community. Along with proclaiming God's Word over our families, we must also share the Compassion of God with other families. We must create the right image of marriage, so that children will pattern their judgment after ours. As an Apostolic Church, we must plant comprehensive marriage ministries to assist couples in building and supporting their relationships. As couples are challenged and nurtured by a variety of support programs, they will be strengthened.

WHERE THE FAULT LIES: WHY AFRICAN-AMERICAN MARRIAGES ARE IN CRISIS

Marriage education should be a vital part of every ministry. Just like preventive ministry, premarital classes should be REQUIRED, in addition to counseling. This will better prepare singles looking to become married. For married couples, learning should be ongoing with a variety of topics geared toward prevention, maintenance, and remedial aims. Evangelism efforts should include an emphasis on targeting the African-American male, since God looks to him to be the head of the household. A safety net of trained counselors with a prophetic ear and a pastor's heart should also be available for those couples experiencing difficulty. Finally, there must be an intercessory team of prayer warriors fasting and praying for the family.

As we are willing to take our set place in the kingdom, God's image will be established in the earth and restoration for the African-American family will be at hand!

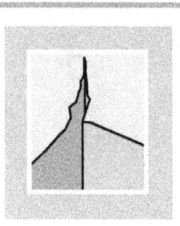

Marriage education should be a vital part of every ministry.

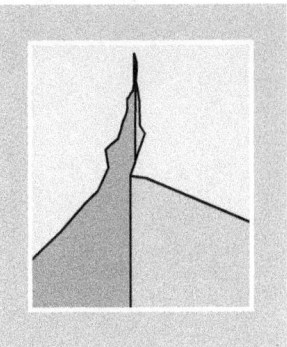

CONCLUSION

The glory of this latter house shall be greater than of the former, saith the LORD of hosts: and in this place will I give peace, saith the LORD of hosts

(Haggai 2:9, KJV).

SOUL FOOD: BREAKING BREAD WITH THE KING

Taking a final look in the book of Esther, we can see that the community that was in crisis is now about to prosper. By chapter 7 the king had sentenced Haman to death and set Mordecai in a place of honor. His latter house was greater than his former house!

This miraculous turnaround was due to Queen Esther's willingness to visit the inner court.

If we take a look back, we find her in Chapter five, ready and willing to go before the king. As she enters, the King is sitting upon his royal throne. When he saw her, he welcomed her. And before she could say a word, the king said, "What do you wish Queen Esther? What is your request? I will give it to you *even if it is* half the kingdom."

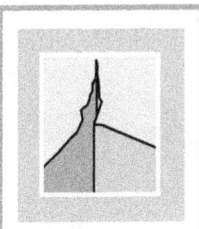

"I will give it to you even if it is half the kingdom."

In conclusion, this is exactly how our King, the King of Kings welcomes us as we enter the inner court. As we stand in His presence. As we enter with praise and thanksgiving and offer a feast of worship unto Him. "He welcomes us." Then, He gazes upon our beauty. Not our outer beauty, but the beauty that comes from those things, that are pleasing in His sight. The beauty that comes from the metamorphosis of His creatures, being made new in Him. As he continues to gaze upon his beloved made in the image of Himself. Our Father desires to do the miraculous. He not only says to us "What is your request, but—"What do you wish my daughter? What do you wish my son? I will give it to you!

Even if it is…

Now, for Queen Esther before she could make her request known; the king offered her half his kingdom—more than she would ever need.

So think about it, how much more can the King of Kings, do than an earthly king for our families? Scripture says, more than we can imagine.

Even if it is…

RESOURCES FOR KINGDOM BUILDING: RECOMMENDATIONS FROM THE AUTHOR

...Yes, A man of knowledge increases strength...

(Proverbs 24:5, NKJV)

For Those Persons Preparing for Marriage

Scripture References:

~Communication
Eph. 4:25-32

~Decision Making
2 Tim. 3:15-17
Heb. 11:23-27

~ Discipline
Prov. 3:11, 12; 13:24;
19:18; 22:6, 15; 23:13;
29:15
1 Cor. 5:1-13; 11:29-34
2 Cor. 2:1-11
Eph. 6:1-4
1 Tim. 4:7
Heb. 12:7-11

~Forgiveness
Prov. 17:9
Matt. 6:14, 15; 18:15-17
Mark 11:25
Luke 17:3-10

~Friendship
Prov. 27:6, 10; 17:9, 17
John 15:13-15

~Humility
Prov. 3:34; 15:33;
16:19; 22:4; 29:23
Gal. 6:1, 2
Phil. 2:1-11
James 4:6, 10
1 Pet. 5:6, 7

~Husband/Wife
Gen. 2:18, 24
Eph. 5:22-23
Col. 3:18-21
1 Pet. 13:1-17
1 Tim. 1:11-15

~Love
Prov. 10:12; 17:19
Matt. 5:44; 22:39, 40
Romans 13:10
1 Cor. 13
1 Pet. 1:22
1 John 4:10, 19; 5:2, 3
2 John 5, 6

Recommended Reading:

~For men:

Jakes, T.D. *So You Call Yourself A Man?* Minneapolis: Bethany House, 1997.

~For women:

Hammond, Michelle. *What To Do Until Love Finds You.* Eugene: Harvest House, 1997.

~Engaged?

McRae, William J. *Preparing for Your Marriage.* Grand Rapids: Zondervan, 1980.

Wright, Norman H. *Before You Remarry.* Eugene: Harvest House, 1988.

Smith, Michael. *Getting Ready for a Lifetime of Love.* Nashville: Broadman & Holman Publishers, 1999.

Notes:

Notes:

For Married Couples

Scripture References:

~Communication
Eph. 4:25-32

~Decision Making:
2 Tim. 3:15-17
Heb. 11:23-27

~Forgiveness
Prov. 17:9
Matt. 6:14, 15; 18:15-17
Mark 11:25
Luke 17:3-10

~Friendship
Prov. 27:6, 10; 17:9, 17
John 15:13- 15

~Humility
Prov. 3:34; 15:33;
16:19; 22:4; 29:23
Gal. 6:1, 2
Phil. 2:1-11
James 4:6, 10
1 Pet. 5:6, 7

~Husband /Wife
Gen. 2:18, 24
Eph. 5:22-23
Col. 3:18-21
1 Pet. 13:1-17
1 Tim. 1:11-15

~Listening
Prov. 5:1, 2, 13;
13:18; 15:31; 18:13

~Love
Prov. 10:12; 17:19
Matt. 5:44; 22:39, 40
Romans 13:10
1 Cor. 13
1 Pet. 1:22
1 John 4:10, 19; 5:2, 3
2 John 5, 6

Recommended Reading:

Blumberg, S., Markman, H., Whitfield, K., Stanley, S. *Fighting for Your African-American Marriage*. San Francisco: Jossey-Bass, 2001.

Wright, Norman S. *Together For Good: A Daily Devotional for Couples*. Eugene: Harvest House, 2000.

Liautaud, Marian Y. *Swatting the Mosquitoes of Marriage*. Grand Rapids: Zondervan, 1994.

Leman, Kevin Dr. *Sex Begins in the Kitchen*. Grand Rapids, Fleming Revell, 1999.

Prince, Derek. *The Marriage Covenant*. Charlotte: Whitaker House, 1978.

Rainbow, Julie. *Standing The Test of Time*. Cleveland: Pilgrim, 2001.

~For men:

Artebum, S. Stoeker, F. *Every Woman's Desire*. Colorado: Random House, 2001.

Smalley, Gary. *If Only He Knew*. Grand Rapids: Zondervan, 1979.

Williams, H. Page. *Doing Myself A Favor: Loving My Wife*. South Plainfield: Bridge, 1994.

Shuler, Clarence. *Keeping Your Wife Your Best Friend*. Chicago: Cool Springs, 2004.

~For women:

Smalley, Gary. *For Better or For Best*. Grand Rapids: Zondervan, 1979.

Hammond, Michelle. *Power of Femininity*. Eugene: Harvest House, 1997.

Notes:

Notes:

For Intercessory Prayer Warriors

Scripture References:

~**Communication**
Eph. 4:25-32

~**Decision Making**
2 Tim. 3:15-17
Heb. 11:23-27

~**Forgiveness**
Prov. 17:9
Matt. 6:14, 15; 18:15-17
Mark 11:25
Luke 17:3-10
Eph.4:32
Col. 3:13
James 5:15
1 John 1:8-10

~**Friendship**
Prov. 27:6, 10; 17:9, 17
John 15:13-15

~**Humility**
Prov. 3:34; 15:33;
16:19; 22:4; 29:23
Gal. 6:1, 2
Phil. 2:1-11
James 4:6, 10
1 Pet. 5:6, 7

~**Husband/Wife**
Gen. 2:18, 24
Eph. 5:22-23
Col. 3:18-21
1 Pet. 13:1-17
1 Tim. 1:11-15

~**Life Dominating Problems**
1 Cor. 6:9-12
Eph. 5:18
Rev. 21:8; 22:15

~**Love**
Prov. 10:12; 17:19
Matt. 5:44; 22:39, 40
Romans 13:10
1 Cor. 13
1 Pet. 1:22
1 John 4:10, 19; 5:2, 3
2 John 5, 6

~**Resentment**
Prov. 26:24-26
Heb. 12:15

Recommended Reading:

White, Thomas. *The Believers' Guide to Spiritual Warfare.* Ann Arbor: Servant Publications, 1990.

Torres, Hector P. *Pulling Down Strongholds.* Colorado: Wagner Institute, 1999.

Wentroble, Barbara. *Prophetic Intercession.* Ventura: Renew Books, 1999.

Frangipane, Frances. *The Three Battlegrounds.* Cedar Rapids: Arrow Publications, 1989.

Notes:

Notes:

For persons separated from their spouse due to marital difficulties

Scripture References:

~Communication
Eph. 4:25-32

~Decision Making
2 Tim. 3:15-17
Heb. 11:23-27

~Depression
Gen. 4:6, 7
Ps. 32, 38, 51
Prov. 18:14
2 Cor. 4:8, 9

~Doubt
James 1:6-8

~Fear
Gen. 3:10
Prov. 10:24; 29:25
Matt. 10:26-31
2 Tim. 1:7
Heb. 2:14, 15
1 Pet. 3:6, 13, 14
1 John 4:18

~Forgiveness
Prov. 17:9
Matt. 6:14, 15; 18:15-17
Mark 11:25
Luke 17:3-10
Eph. 4:32
Col. 3:13
James 5:15
1 John 1:8-10

~Grief
Prov. 14:13; 15:13
Eph. 4:30
1 Thess. 4:13-18

~Humility
Prov. 3:34; 15:33; 16:19; 22:4; 29:23
Gal. 6:1, 2
Phil. 2: 1-11
James 4:6, 10
1 Pet. 5:6, 7

~Listening
Prov. 5:1, 2, 13; 13:18; 15:31; 18:13

~Love
Prov. 10:12; 17:19
Matt. 5:44; 22:39, 40
Romans 13:10
1 Cor. 13
1 Pet. 1:22
1 John 4:10, 19; 5:2, 3
2 John 5, 6

~Peace
Prov. 3:1, 2; 16:7
John 14:27
Romans 5:1; 12:18; 14:19
Philippians 4:6-9
Col. 3:15
Hebrew 12:14

~Resentment
Prov. 26:24-26
Heb. 12:15

Recommended Reading:

Chapman, Gary. *Wounded Marriages Can Be Healed: Hope for the Separated.* Chicago: Moody Press, 1996.

Seamands, David A. *Healing for Damaged Emotions.* Colorado: Victor, 2002.

Dobson, Dr. James C. *New Hope for Families in Crisis: Love Must be Tough* World Books, 1993.

Meyer, Joyce. *Life Without Strife: How God Can Heal and Restore Troubled Relationships.* Lake Mary: Creation House, *2000.*

Carder, Dave. *Torn Asunder.* Chicago: Moody Press, 1995.

Notes:

Notes:

Notes:

Notes:

BOOKNOTES

INTRODUCTION
FOR A TIME SUCH AS THIS: STATING THE CASE FOR AFRICAN-AMERICAN MARRIAGE

1. Whitehead, Barbara D. (1996). *The divorce culture*. New York: Random House, 44.

2. Frazier, Franklin E. (1939). *The negro family in the united states*. Chicago: University of Chicago Press.

3. Cherlin, Andrew J. (Spring 1998). Marriage and marital dissolution among black americans. *Journal of Comparative Family Studies, v. 29 no 1* Retrieved November 27, 2002, from http://newfirstsearch.oclc.org

4. Besharov, Douglas J. & West, Andrew. (2002). *African-American marriage patterns*. Hoover Press: Thernstrom.

5. Ibid.

6. McKinnon, Jessie. (2003). The black population in the united states: march 2002. *U.S. Census Bureau.* Retrieved July 10, 2003, from http://www.census.gov/prod/2003pubs/p20-541.pdf

DISCOVERING THE FAULT LINE
A LOOK AT HISTORY

1. Strong, James E. (1890). Hebrew and chaldee dictionary in *Strong's exhaustive concordance of the bible*. Nashville: Holman Bible Publishers, entry # 8356.

CHAPTER 1
AN OPEN DOOR: SLAVERY

1. Archer, Gleason L. (1982). *Encyclopedia of bible difficulties*. Grand Rapids: Zondervan Corporation.

2. Schneider, Dorothy & Carl. (2000). *Slavery in america: from colonial times to the civil war.* New York: Facts on File Inc.

3. Time Life. (1993). *African-American voices of triumph: Vol. Perseverance.* Richmond: Time Life Inc.

4. Schneider.

5. Time Life.

6. Equiano, Olaudah, b. (1969). *Equiano's travels: his autobiography: the Interesting narrative of the life of Olaudah Equiano or Gustavus Vassa, The African.* London: Heinemann, 16.

7. Rasmussen, Kent R. ed. (2001). *The african american encyclopedia-* 2nd ed. New York: Marshall Cavendish.

8. Globe Book Editors. (1992). *The African American Experience.* Englewood Cliffs: Globe Book Co.

9. Fogel, Robert W. & Engerman, Stanley L. (1974). T*ime on the cross: the economics of american negro slavery.* Canada: Little Brown & Co.

10. Pederson, Jay & Estell, Kenneth. (2001). *Reference library of black america almanac.* New York: Gale Group.

11. Rasmussen.

12. Metzger, Bruce M. & Coogan Michael D. (2001). *The oxford essential guide to Ideas & issues of the bible.* New York: Oxford University Press, 462.

13. The Stonesong Press, Inc. and The New York Public Library. *African American Desk Reference.* (1999). New York: John Wiley & Sons, Inc.

14. *African American history.* (n.d)..Retrieved April 2, 2003 from http://encarta.msn. com

15. Pederson.

CHAPTER 2 - POINT OF ENTRY: THE SLAVE MARRIAGE

1. Elkins, Stanley. (1976). *Slavery a problem in american institutional and intellectual life. Chicago:* University of Chicago Press, 54.
2. Genovese, Eugene D. (1976). *Roll Jordan roll: the world the slaves made* New York: Random House.
3. Sterling, Dorothy. (1984). *We are your sisters: black women in the nineteenth century.* New York: W.W. Norton Co.
4. "Plantation Courtship", *Southern Workman XXIV* (Jan. 1895), Hampton Folklore Society, 14-15.
5. Ibid, 15.
6. Ibid.
7. Bibb, Henry. (1849). *Narrative of the life and adventures of Henry Bibb: an American slavery.* In African American Odyssey. [http://memory.loc.gov/ammem/aap/aahome.html] [E444.B58] (January 15, 2004), 36.
8. Ibid, 37.
9. Schneider.
10. Ibid, 86.
11. Blassingame, John W. ed. (1977). *Slave testimony.* Baton Rouge: Louisiana State University Press, 592.
12. Cole, Harriet. (1993). *Jumping the broom.* Ontario: Fitzhenry & Whiteside Ltd.
13. Kelley, Robin D.G. & Lewis, Earl. (2000). *A history of African-Americans.* New York: Oxford Press.
14. Bibb, 40.
15. Will, Thomas E., Weddings on contested grounds: slave marriage in the antebellum south. *The Historian.* (Fall 1999), 99-117.

16. Kolchin, Peter. (1993). *American Slavery 1619-1877.* Canada: Harper Collins.
17. Schneider.
18. Bibb, 42.
19. Nichols, Charles, ed. (1972). *Black men in chains: narratives by escaped slaves.* Providence: Brown University, 132.
20. Kelley and Lewis, 187.
21. Ball, Charles. (1859). *Fifty years in chains, the life of an American slave.* New York: H. Dayton.
22. Will.
23. Time Life.
24. Will.
25. Jacobs, Harriet Ann. (1860). *Incidents in the Life of a Slave Girl.* Written by Herself. Boston: Published for the author. Electronic Edition: Call #VC326.92 JI7i (North Carolina Collection, UNC-Chapel Hill), 61.
26. Ibid.
27. Loguen, J. W. Rev. (1859) *The Reverend J. W. Loguen as a slave and as a freeman.* Syracuse: by the author, 223.
28. Brown, William Wells. (1857). *Narrative of William W. Brown a fugitive slave.* Boston: by the author, 85, 87.
29. Bibb, 36.
30. Malone, Anne Patton. (1992). Sweet Chariot. Chapel Hill: University of North Carolina Press.

CHAPTER 3
A SPIRITUAL ASSAULT: FORCED TERMINATION

1. Lester, Julius. (1968). *To be a slave.* New York: Dial Press.

2. *Slave marriages*. (n.d.). Retrieved December 18. 2002 from http://www.spartacus.schoolnet.co.uk/usasmarriage.htm
3. Dennis, Ethel R. (1970). *The black people of America*. New Haven: Readers Press: McGraw Hill.
4. Time Life.
5. Dennis, 66.
6. Ball.
7. Lester, 48.
8. Ball, Charles, 12.
9. Brown, W. W.
10. Ball, 35.
11. Grandy, Moses. (1843). *Narrative of the Life of Moses Grandy; Late a Slave in the United States of America*. London. Electronic Edition: Call 3 C326.92 G75 (North Carolina Collection), 16.
12. Brown, Henry Box. (1851). Narrative *of Henry Box Brown*. Boston, 56.
13. Ibid.
14. http://www.civilwar-150.com/just-from-slavery--voice-of-the-fugitive-june-4-1851-page-2.
15. Northup, Solomon. (1854). *Twelve years a slave*. Auburn: Derby and Miller.
16. Gutman, Herbert. (1976). *The black family in slavery and freedom 1750-1925*. New York: Random House, 20-21.
17. Raboteau, Albert J. (1978). *Slave religion*. New York: Oxford.
18. Bibb, 152.
19. Brown, 56-57.
20. Swint, H.L. ed. (1966). *Dear ones at home: letters from the contraband camps*. Nashville: Vanderbilt University Press, 242-43.

CHAPTER 4
CAUGHT IN THE CROSSFIRE: GRIEVING WITH GOD FOR THE CHILDREN

1. King, Wilma. (1995). *Stolen childhood.* Bloomington: Indiana University press, 6.
2. Bibb, 44.
3. Blassingame, (1977), 594.
4. Genovese.
5. *Reproductive choice.* (n.d.). Retrieved July 23, 2003, from http//www.gwu.edu/~medusa/reproductive.html
6. King.
7. *Reproductive choice.*
8. Rawick, George P. ed., (1972). *The American slave: a composite autobiography* vol # 6 Westpoint: Greenwood Publications.
9. Time Life, 32.
10. Genovese.
11. Ball, 78.
12. Adams, John Quincy, 1845-. (1872). *Narrative of the life of John Quincy Adams, when in slavery and now as a freeman.* Harrisburg: Seig, Printer, 6.
13. Bibb, 43.
14. Ball, 10.
15. Ibid.

CHAPTER 5
PSYCHOLOGICAL WARFARE: THE PSYCHOLOGICAL EFFECTS ON WOMANHOOD AND MANHOOD

1. Douglas, Frederick. (1968). *My bondage and my freedom 1855.* New York: Arno Press, 221.

2. Ball.
3. Northup, 60, 61.
4. Protestant Episcopal Church in the Confederate States. (1862). *Catechism, to* be taught orally to those who cannot read; designed especially for *the instruction of the slaves.* Electronic Edition: Call # VC p238 p96c 1862 (North Carolina Collection, UNC-CH)
5. Bibb.
6. Gutman.
7. Ibid, 79.

CHAPTER 6
SAFE HOUSES: SPIRITUAL SONGS

1. Adams.
2. Raboteau. Also, Ball.
3. Bibb, 199.
4. Lester, 10.
5. Sellers, James B. (1950). *Slavery in Alabama.* Alabama: University Press, 300.
6. Boschman, LaMar. (1986). *The prophetic song.* Shippenburg: Revival Press, 3.
7. Ibid, 5.
8. Douglas, Frederick. (1960). *Narrative of the life of Frederick Douglas.* Cambridge: Belknap, 38.
9. Brown, W.W., 51, 52.
10. *Slave songs transcend sorrow* (n.d.). Retrieved July 21, 2003, from http//www.Gospelcom.net/chi/GLIMPSEF/glimpses/glmps089.shtml
11. Brown, 52.
12. Box Brown, ix.
13. Metzer, 462.

AFTERSHOCKS
THE IMPACT OF SLAVERY ON TODAY'S COUPLE

1. Du Bois, W.E. Burghardt. (1908). *The negro American family.* New York: Negro University Press; Frazier, (1939).

2. Patterson, Orlando. (1998). *Rituals of Blood.* Washington:Civitas Counterpoint.

CHAPTER 7
BROKEN IMAGES: STEREOTYPES THAT DESTROY ONENESS

1. Cazenave, Noel A. and Smith, Rita. *Gender differences in the perception of black male-female relationships and stereotypes.* Black Families: Interdisiplinary Perspectives. New Brunswick: Transaction Books (1991).

CHAPTER 8
OPTING FOR FREEDOM: A WORD ON DELIVERANCE

No References.

RESTORING THE FOUNDATION

No References.

www.ingramcontent.com/pod-product-compliance
Lightning Source LLC
Chambersburg PA
CBHW051801040426
42446CB00007B/461